HERITAGE

Vegetables

HERITAGE

Vegetables

The
Gardener's
Guide
to Cultivating
Diversity

Gaia Books Limited

SUE STICKLAND

Foreword by Alan Gear of the Henry Doubleday Research Association

Photographs by David Cavagnaro

LEFT: *Traditional varieties of Alliums can be grown without difficulty in most climates, including red- or white-skinned onions, pearl onions and shallots, leeks and many different types of garlic.*

A GAIA ORIGINAL
Books from Gaia celebrate the vision of Gaia, the self-sustaining living Earth, and seek to help readers live in greater personal and planetary harmony.

Editor   Charlie Ryrie
Designer   Kitty Crossley
Managing Editor   Pip Morgan
Production   Lyn Kirby

First published in the United Kingdom in 1998 by
Gaia Books Ltd, 66 Charlotte St, London W1P 1LR
and 20 High St, Stroud, Glos GL5 1AS

ISBN 1 85675 033 7

A catalogue record of this book is available from the British Library.

Images reproduced in Singapore by Master Image
Printed and bound in Hong Kong by Dai Nippon

10 9 8 7 6 5 4 3 2 1

PUBLISHER'S ACKNOWLEDGEMENTS

Gaia Books would like to thank the HDRA, especially Alan Gear and Bob Sherman and his team for their support and helpful suggestions all the way through this project. Thanks also to Nancy Arrowsmith from Arche Noah, and to Kent Whealy at Seed Savers Exchange. A special thank you goes to David Cavagnaro for providing wonderful photographs and invaluable information, and thanks to him and his family for their fantastic hospitality while the book was getting underway. We should like to thank all the organisations and seed suppliers in the UK and Europe for supplying us with information and, in many cases, taking time to deal with our queries. Without all their work and dedication, this book could not exist.

Thanks to Colin Wilkin for the artwork on pages 22–23 and page 53; Charlie Ryrie for photographs on pages 90 and 95, and Lyn Bresler for preparing the Index.

THE AUTHOR

Sue Stickland has worked as a professional gardener for 20 years. She was Head Gardener with the Henry Doubleday Research Association (HDRA) when they set up Ryton organic gardens near Coventry, and there became involved with the HDRA's Heritage Vegetable collection. She is an established author, writing books and articles on organic and related topics, and was one of the presenters of the ground-breaking Channel 4 series *All Muck and Magic?* Her books include *G is for Eco-Garden*; *Greenhouses: natural vegetables, fruit and flowers all the year round*; *Organic Gardening* and *The Small Ecological Garden*.

THE CONSULTANT

Alan Gear joined the Henry Doubleday Research Association, Europe's leading organic organisation, in 1973, and has been its Chief Executive since 1985. He is an accomplished writer, lecturer and broadcaster and also presented Channel 4's popular organic gardening series *All Muck and Magic?*

THE PHOTOGRAPHER

David Cavagnaro is a naturalist, plantsman, writer and photographer whose words and pictures have appeared in books and magazines worldwide. Arriving at Seed Savers Exchange in Iowa, US, 12 years ago, on a photographic assignment for Organic Gardener magazine, he was so inspired that he stayed to help. For eight years he was the curator at the SSE gardens, and he probably knows more than anyone about their range of vegetables, having grown and photographed many of them.

AUTHOR'S ACKNOWLEDGEMENTS

My thanks to all the seed suppliers and seed savers' networks who so willingly provided information and advice for this book; in particular to Bob Sherman at HDRA for answering my numerous queries so quickly and efficiently, and also to Nancy Arrowsmith from Arche Noah, Peter Erlandsson from SESAM, Ray Warner from Thomas Etty, Brian Haynes from Kings Seeds, and Reinhold Kramer from Kutchengarten.

Thanks also to Patrick Mulvaney from Intermediate Technology, Joy Larkcom, Anthony Jacobsohn, Bergitta Ramert and Anemette Olesen for their technical help, and to Margi Lennartsson, Jane White, Helen Liebsher and Mr T. Brydon for their help with translation.

Finally my thanks to Dave for tolerating the house littered with foreign seed catalogues and my complete absorption in heritage vegetables over the last nine months.

Sue Stickland July 1997

CONTENTS

FOREWORD

The first inhabitants of the British Isles had very little choice of plants to eat – just a few wild ancestors of crops like carrots, celery and cabbages, plus species such as marsh samphire that still remain largely unexploited.

When the Romans invaded they brought with them seeds of radishes, onions, parsnips, peas, beetroot and other non-indigenous vegetables. Peripatetic Jews and Arabs introduced cauliflowers and aubergines with other vegetables native to the Middle East. More new crops – potatoes, beans and tomatoes – arrived via the pioneers returning from the New World. Such a process still continues: Chinese and Oriental salad crops, for example, have become well-established in the Northern European diet in little more than a decade or two.

There is little to connect our present-day carrots visibly with their wild counterparts. The latter have insignificant white roots which, though edible, hold little culinary promise. The way they have evolved into a substantial food crop is testament to the countless individuals who, over the centuries, have saved the seeds from selected plants to produce the carrots we enjoy today.

It has become common practice to buy vegetable seeds from seed companies, yet such businesses did not exist until the 16th century. Before then, every farmer and gardener was responsible for saving their own seeds. They were precious currency, to be handed down through generations. In industrialised countries this practice has largely disappeared, but it is still commonplace in many parts of Eastern Europe and the developing world.

During the 19th century, vegetable growing was enthusiastically practised by all strata of society, from head gardeners of country estates through to city-dwelling working men cultivating allotments. The market for seed consisted largely of people growing crops for their own consumption, not for commercial sales, so Victorian seedsmen used to breed varieties to satisfy gardeners – at the time there was no great division between the needs of professional growers and gardeners. It is only during the latter part of the 20th century that the varieties grown by farmers for supermarkets and food processors have diverged significantly from those of the amateur market – with devastating consequences.

In recent years the multiple retailers have at last begun to appreciate that flavour is important to consumers, but qualities such as uniformity of appearance and freedom from blemishes are still more valuable to them. Supermarkets, with their long supply chains and centralised distribution systems, also require produce sufficiently robust to withstand frequent handling and lengthy journeys – hence the virtual impossibility of finding a tomato with a thin skin! Seedsmen have typically responded to the financial incentives of the commercial growers' market by concentrating on appropriate varieties. There is a comparatively small market for the traditional, open-pollinated varieties suitable for gardeners, so they have progressively disappeared from catalogues.

As if commercial pressures threatening our old varieties were not enough, in the mid-1970s officialdom dealt a further appalling blow – the passing of the Seed (National List of Varieties) Act 1973. This closely followed Britain's accession to the EC (*see page 65*). Since then, all vegetable seeds for sale have had to be included on an official UK list or a composite EC register. In order to qualify for registration, every variety must demonstrate that it is distinct (different from all other varieties), uniform (all plants should be more or less identical), and stable (breeds true).

In 1980, more than 1,500 distinctly named varieties were banned for being supposed 'synonyms', *i.e.* identical to other varieties but with different names. Yet our own research at the time showed that only a third fell into that category – the remainder were originals, but unwanted by the commercial sector. HDRA campaigned continuously against the Seed Act throughout the 1970s but was unable to get any relaxation of the rules.

So why does it matter so much if vegetable varieties disappear? Though we are obviously concerned at the curtailing of the basic freedom of gardeners to grow vegetables of their choice in their own gardens, there is a

much bigger issue at stake. It is all very well discarding varieties that have no obvious place in today's market, but who knows what will be needed tomorrow? We cannot tell when a new pest or disease will strike, or what qualities or characteristics may be required in an era of climate change. Old varieties contain irreplaceable genetic material that could be vital to future breeding programmes – we discard them at our peril.

At least our warnings on this score were heeded, and in 1980 we persuaded Oxfam to fund the building of a vegetable gene bank, where varieties could be kept safely under deep freeze conditions. We had already set up the Heritage Seed Library, in 1975, as an initiative to get heritage varieties into the hands of gardeners. If it was illegal to sell unregistered seeds, we decided we would give them away in return for an annual member-ship fee. This just about upheld the letter of the law, even if it broke the spirit! From small beginnings the Library has now grown to a thriving operation with more than 7,000 members and over 600 unique varieties of vegetable seeds, many featuring in this book.

The seeds, including potato tubers, are grown at HDRA's headquarters at Ryton-on-Dunsmore, and at its gardens at Yalding, near Maidstone in Kent. Some varieties are grown out-of-doors, but the majority are cultivated in polytunnels. Since this harvest could not possibly meet the demand, a network of over 230 volunteer 'Seed Guardians' now exists; each Guardian undertakes to save seed from plants of a specific variety and returns it to us for distribution. In 1996 we expanded our volunteer network by recruiting 'Seed Sleuths'. These amateur historians research local newspapers and other archives to find contemporary accounts of 'new' seeds introduced by Victorian seedsmen, to shed light on the history of varieties.

Perhaps our most famous variety is the crimson-flowered broad bean. It was given to us by a Miss Cutbush, an elderly spinster in Kent, whose ancestors ran a market garden on the outskirts of London at the turn of the century. From just four seeds, it has 'bulked up' until it is now enjoyed by thousands of gardeners the world over, its security assured through the simple act of giving it away.

The Martock bean, an HSL variety (*see page 109*) which we believe to date back to the Middle Ages, has characteristics that do not at first seem to recommend it at all. Named after a small Somerset village, it was donated by a former Bishop of Bath and Wells who found it in the Palace gardens. Although it resembles a small broad bean, it is not eaten fresh, but harvested when it is bullet-hard to be used as winter protein in soups. Nothing very special had been noted about the bean apart from its ancient history until recently, when researchers found it to be a martyr to blackfly, a serious pest to some crops. So Martock makes an excellent sacrificial crop – grow it next to other crops and pests will be lured away, avoiding the need for pesticides!

Who knows what other similar useful traits remain undiscovered in the hundreds of heritage varieties that are the subject of this book? Fortunately the tide of public opinion is now turning in favour of keeping our priceless vegetable heritage alive. In 1995, an appeal to 'Adopt a Veg', launched by HDRA's patron The Prince of Wales, produced a phenomenal media response: over the ensuing twelve months we recorded more than 50 national and local radio and TV bulletins, and over 100 articles appeared in the press. Even the EC has at last indicated plans to repeal its repressive seed laws.

Our next aim is to secure funding to enable us to repatriate, and return to public cultivation, those long-lost vegetable varieties that were taken by emigrants to the United States and the former colonies in earlier centuries, and which survive to this day in public and private seed collections.

In the meantime, you can show your support for heritage seeds by growing and enjoying many of the superb examples described so graphically, and with such enthusiasm, in this book.

Alan Gear · July 1997
Chief Executive, HDRA, Ryton Organic Gardens

PART

1

Variety,
the Essence of Life

❶
OUR VEGETABLE HERITAGE

ABOVE: *Potatoes come in many guises, and thousands of varieties exist, each with distinctive qualities and appearance.*

LEFT: *This small selection of European heritage lettuces hints at the wide diversity of colours and leaf shapes.*

Dazzling displays of cleanly scrubbed and brightly lit supermarket vegetables deceive us with their size and colour. A display in a New York store will be almost identical to one in London, or in Paris or in Stockholm – and it will be much the same in January as in June. You will see the same types of vegetables, and they are likely to be exactly the same varieties. Tomatoes are most often round and red; potatoes are either 'reds' or 'whites', and a carrot – well, a carrot is just a carrot. Seasonal produce and local varieties appear to have vanished, and with them choice, and very often taste.

If you can grow your own vegetables, you are immediately better off. You have to harvest seasonally, and seed catalogues give you more choice than any supermarket shelf. However, you need to search out your suppliers carefully; the continuing drive for homogeneity means major seed companies offer far shorter lists than a few decades ago. Moreover, many of the new entries are modern hybrids, with few significant differences between varieties, and with qualities which may be quite irrelevant to a gardener. Conventional seed suppliers are rarely small local businesses any more, but have increasingly become part of large corporations.

Yet an amazing diversity of vegetables does still exist, in ranges of shape, size, colour, cooking quality and taste that most of us have never dreamt of, and with differences in cold-tolerance, harvest times, and resistance to pests and diseases that are of immense value to gardeners and growers. Only a handful of these varieties can be found in shops, or even seed catalogues, today.

Potatoes are one of the best examples of this significant impoverishment; they are a staple crop of world importance, and Europe and the US are among the chief producers. However, most commercial potato growers in these countries will plant just two or three varieties each year, and there is a good chance that neighbouring farmers will be planting the same ones. In the UK in the early 1990s, the ten most commonly grown potatoes occupied around 70 per cent of the total area put down to the crop. These same varieties are obviously the ones that are most likely to be found in shops and supermarkets, and inevitably they are going to be the ones most likely to be sold as seed potatoes to gardeners. This ever narrowing base is despite the fact that at least 230 varieties were available in 1996 through US and Canadian catalogues, and 150 varieties via UK

TOMATOES

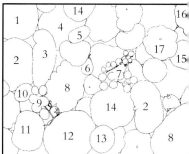

1. Pink Brandywine

2. Evergreen

3. Opalka Paste

4. Pineapple

5. Red Plum

6. Red Pear

7. Red Currant

8. Zapotec

9. Broad Ripple Yellow Currant

10. Yellow Pear

11. Golden Queen

12. Big Rainbow

13. Tigerella

14. White Snowball

15. Stuffer

16. Great White

17. Costoluto Genovese

seed suppliers. Many more are in the hands of amateur collectors and seed saving groups in their respective countries.

These monocultures in developed countries contrast strongly with the traditional ways of peasant farmers in the Andes. Here it is not uncommon to find at least 45 distinct potato varieties growing in one valley and it has been estimated that Andean farmers cultivate some 3,000 different varieties in total, potatoes of varied shapes and a whole spectrum of colours from black to bright yellow.

The tomato is another crop with seemingly endless diversity – so often reduced by commercial growers and supermarkets to smooth round red fruits. Most of us have tasted smaller, sweet cherry tomatoes, and seen the occasional yellow tomato or fleshy beefsteak type on the shelves of some stores, or among the many new F1 hybrids in popular seed catalogues. But this is just the tip of a largely hidden iceberg of diversity. Tomatoes can be red, pink, orange, yellow, black, green or white, and streaks are not uncommon. They may be egg-shaped or

ABOVE: *Originating in Russia, Black Krim tomatoes are thin-skinned, sweet and incredibly juicy.*

pear-shaped, or have ridges and bulges. Some are very solid and others almost hollow, they may be bitter or sweet, and have numerous different uses in the kitchen.

Size, shape, colour and taste are a few of the obvious ways in which tomatoes can vary. Other characteristics, such as the ability to set (form fruit) in cold conditions, or resistance to fungal diseases, are equally important to growers and gardeners, but can easily go unnoticed. In the mid 1990s well over 600 varieties were commercially available via seed suppliers in the US and Canada, 150 in the UK, over 400 offered by the US network Seed Savers Exchange, and 2,500 varieties kept as seed in the gene bank in Gatersleben, Germany.

This vast diversity of crops has co-evolved over hundreds of years, along with the people who cultivated and used them. It is fitting that we should regard them as our heritage, and look upon the individual varieties as heirlooms – something precious beyond monetary value. The problem with heritage vegetables is that, unlike gold watches or bibles, plants and their seeds have a short life. In order to survive they have to be grown and cared for.

Many old varieties still in existence are, quite literally, family heirlooms, their seeds handed down from one generation to the next, never coming into the hands of the commercial seed companies. At one time, saving seeds and passing them on was a matter of survival – otherwise there would be no seed to sow the following year, no crop to harvest and no food to eat. American Indians, or peasant farmers in any culture, would have taken this for granted. However, by the second half of the 20th century, only a small minority of growers were saving their own seed; most relied instead on the seed companies. Fortunately, a few families and communities have carried on their traditional seed saving ways, and a large number

BOOTHBY'S BLOND CUCUMBER

The distinctive cucumber, Boothby's Blond, was grown for several generations by the Boothby family in Maine, USA, but only became commercially available in the mid 1990s, when it was taken up by a couple of small US seed companies with an interest in old varieties.

Short, oval fruits have warty creamy-yellow skin and very sweet and delicate flesh.

Boothby's Blond is ideal for cooler climates, as long as it is grown in a sunny position.

SUMMER SQUASH

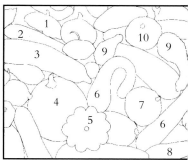

1. Bennings Green Tint

2. Golden Zucchini

3. Bulgarian Summer

4. Ronde de Nice

5. White Bush Scallop

6. Cocozelle

7. Mandan

8. Caserta

9. Early Summer Crookneck

10. Weisser Patisson

of the old varieties do still exist. Many of these have a history that can be traced back well over a hundred years, others may date from early this century; all are valuable.

In the US, one important heirloom is a bronze-tinged leafy lettuce, Grandpa Admires (*see right*). It was the donation of seeds of this old variety that motivated the establishment of Seed Savers Exchange. A favourite UK heirloom is a crimson-flowered broad bean. An elderly lady, who had seen her father growing the beans throughout his life, passed on seeds to the Henry Doubleday Research Asociation seedsaving group in 1978. Although crimson-flowered broad beans were recorded as long ago as 1778, and despite their value as food and ornament – the flowers are highly attractive – they never made it into commercial seed catalogues. Without such a gift they would have become extinct, along with their history and unique genetic make-up.

Some much-loved old varieties developed as the result of traditional plant breeding programmes by small seed companies. Although not heirlooms in the sense of being kept alive by families, they are also vitally important. Many of them, such as Scarlet Emperor runner bean, or Golden Bantam corn, are now being labelled by seed merchants as inferior, and are at risk of being completely replaced by modern hybrids (*see page 41*).

In discovering traditional varieties, it is easy to get caught up in nostalgia and delve deeper and deeper into the past. But these plants are also a fundamental part of the future. Using the words 'heritage' and 'heirloom' recognises that we are responsible for preserving the wealth of vegetable diversity that still exists – not by keeping them as museum pieces, but by growing them, using them, and passing them on.

GRANDPA ADMIRES (*above*)

George Admire was a civil war veteran born in 1822. In 1977 his granddaughter, 90 year old Cloe Lowrey, gave some of his lettuce seed to Kent and Diane Whealy. This gift, added to two varieties of seeds passed down through generations of Diane's family, inspired the Whealys to set up Seed Savers Exchange, a network dedicated to preserving the genetic diversity of the world's food crops through saving heirlooms and endangered varieties.

ANDEAN POTATOES

In the Peruvian valleys, there is a potato variety covered in little knobs which the native people are said to call 'the potato that makes the young bride weep'.

A new bride can be sent away if she is not nimble enough to peel one of these potatoes without slicing off a single knob.

The origins of crops

Modern researchers do not always agree about the exact origins of individual crops, or where they were first developed. But the concept that crops have specific centres of diversity is an important one. These centres are nearly all in tropical or subtropical regions, often close to, and isolated by, mountains, lakes and rivers. These regions have wide variations in soil type and climate, and usually encompass different peoples with varying needs, all factors which force different adaptations of the crops.

Most of our important crops came originally from the Near East, Northern China, and parts of Southern America, where there is an enormous genetic variation in the crops, and their wild relatives. Central Asia is thought to be the centre of origin of carrots, spinach, onion, peas, and broad beans (*Vicia spp*); South America is deemed the source of squashes, corn, potatoes, tomatoes, and French, runner and Lima beans (*Phaseolus spp*). Such areas are often referred to as Vavilov centres after the Russian scientist who first proposed the idea.

Secondary centres of diversity are typically regions where a crop was introduced very early on, and then had a chance to develop many varied forms. For example, many of our cultivated tomatoes originated in Mexico and Central America, yet the crop is descended from wild species from the Andes, where the greatest numbers of wild forms are still found. One theory suggests that tomatoes travelled to Mexico as a weed in corn crops.

Very few vegetables are indigenous to North America or Northern Europe. Most have been brought in by travellers – conquering armies, refugees, explorers, slaves, immigrants, missionaries or even wildlife.

CROOKNECK SQUASH
(*CUCURBITA PEPO*)

Bulb-shaped squashes with narrow curved necks were amongst the first vegetables to be taken back to Europe from South America by the Spanish. Old varieties, such as Yellow Crookneck, continue to be popular today. These are summer squashes, best eaten fresh from the vine when the fruits are about 15cm (6in) long. The skin becomes bumpy and warted on larger fruits.

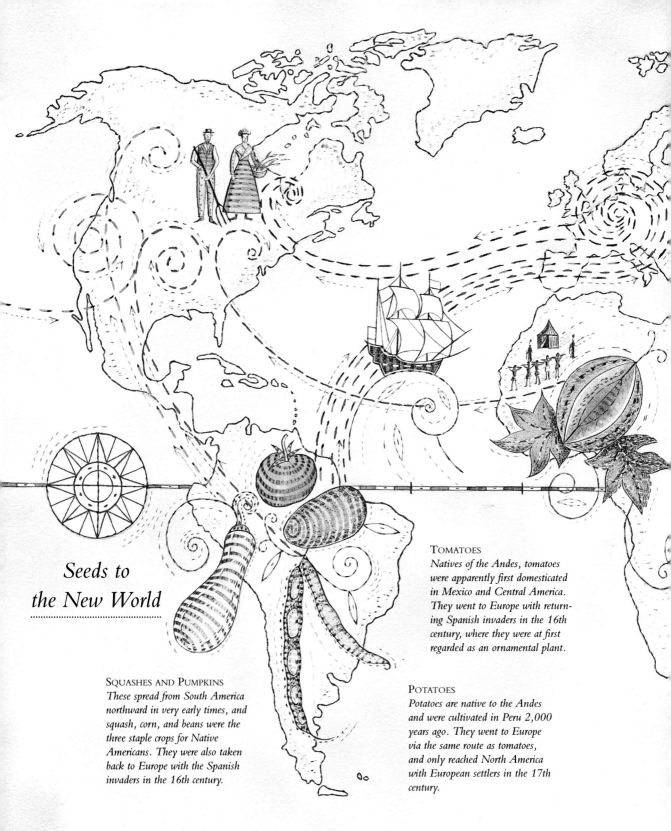

Seeds to the New World

SQUASHES AND PUMPKINS

These spread from South America northward in very early times, and squash, corn, and beans were the three staple crops for Native Americans. They were also taken back to Europe with the Spanish invaders in the 16th century.

TOMATOES

Natives of the Andes, tomatoes were apparently first domesticated in Mexico and Central America. They went to Europe with returning Spanish invaders in the 16th century, where they were at first regarded as an ornamental plant.

POTATOES

Potatoes are native to the Andes and were cultivated in Peru 2,000 years ago. They went to Europe via the same route as tomatoes, and only reached North America with European settlers in the 17th century.

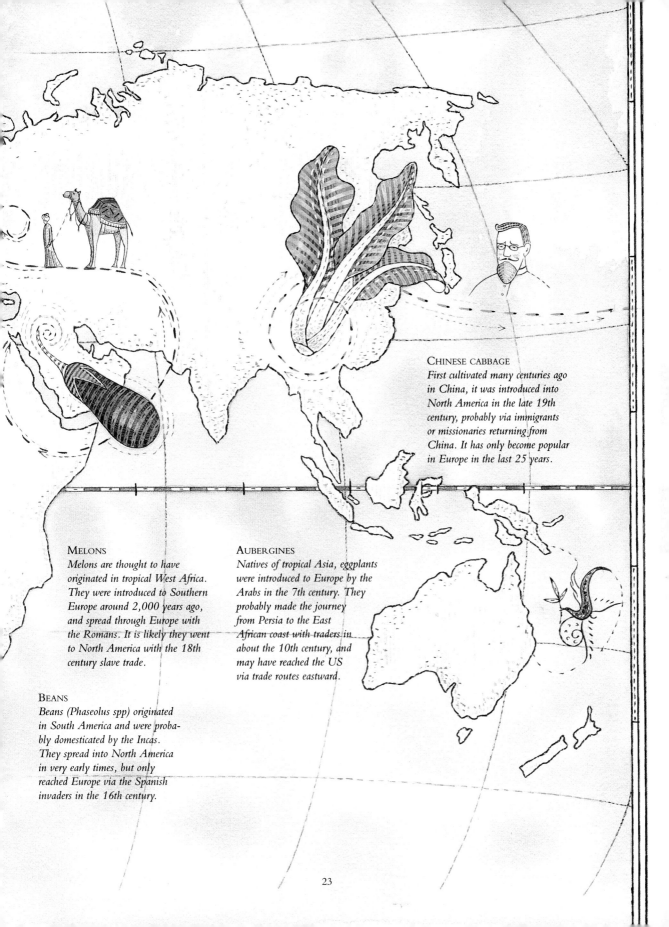

CHINESE CABBAGE

First cultivated many centuries ago in China, it was introduced into North America in the late 19th century, probably via immigrants or missionaries returning from China. It has only become popular in Europe in the last 25 years.

MELONS

Melons are thought to have originated in tropical West Africa. They were introduced to Southern Europe around 2,000 years ago, and spread through Europe with the Romans. It is likely they went to North America with the 18th century slave trade.

AUBERGINES

Natives of tropical Asia, eggplants were introduced to Europe by the Arabs in the 7th century. They probably made the journey from Persia to the East African coast with traders in about the 10th century, and may have reached the US via trade routes eastward.

BEANS

Beans (Phaseolus spp) originated in South America and were proba-bly domesticated by the Incas. They spread into North America in very early times, but only reached Europe via the Spanish invaders in the 16th century.

Vegetable travellers

Crops spread outwards from their centres of diversity, first reaching the areas that were easily accessible by land or by short sea trips. Peas, for example, which originated in Asia, were found in Northern Europe in prehistoric times: archaeologists have discovered seeds in excavations of Swiss Lake dwellings dating back to the Bronze Age, and two early Iron Age storage pits full of peas have been found in South East England. Broad beans were among the first crops known to have travelled to Northern Europe, where prehistoric people would probably also have eaten a type of leafy non-heading cabbage, since wild cabbage is native to the coastal areas of Western Europe.

The beet family is another crop with European origins, and wild sea beets on the Mediterranean and Atlantic coasts were domesticated very long ago. They were originally developed for their green and red leaves, giving rise to the spinach beets and chards that we know today. It was only in Roman times that more palatable cabbages, and other staple vegetables such as parsnips, onions and carrots arrived in Western Europe. A few more exotic crops such as melons and cucumber were also introduced during this period, and others came with the Arabs and Jews a few centuries later.

Separated from Europe by the ocean, the development of vegetables in the Americas was entirely independent. Squash, corn (maize), and beans (runner, French and lima beans) were cultivated in South America in ancient times. These important crops are referred to as the Three Sisters of traditional American agriculture. Intermixed, they protected and upheld each other as they grew: the beans provided nitrogen for growth; the corn stems provided supports for the beans to climb; and the long sprawling vines and large leaves of the squashes kept the soil beneath cool and moist for the other two sisters. When the crops were

LEFT: *This attractive heirloom chard – known as Ruby or Rhubarb chard – is descended from a deep red variety which was once admired by Aristotle. Many early varieties of vegetable exhibited more intense colours than those commonly in cultivation today.*

harvested, they provided a diet balanced in carbohydrates and vegetable protein.

There are records of the cultivation of tomatoes and peppers in Central and South America as early as the 5th century BC; vivid portrayals of potatoes on early ceramics found in Peru suggest that the vegetable had an almost god-like status.

Europe and America originally had very few crops in common, and the year 1492, when Columbus first sailed to America, was a critical one. After that date, the range of vegetable crops on both continents increased enormously. Along with gold and other Inca treasures, the Spanish invaders of South America took potatoes, tomatoes, beans, squashes and peppers back to Europe.

These vegetable curiosities were not always readily accepted: runner beans, for example, were first grown purely for their scarlet flowers, and their edible qualities dismissed. Potatoes suffered through the Europeans' ignorance, as few were aware of the poisonous qualities of the foliage, nor that, to be safe, tubers for eating must be kept in the dark. Initially, therefore, some people fell ill and died, which did not enhance the potato's reception!

Italian vegetables

Italy is in the Mediterranean centre of diversity. Although few vegetable species actually came originally from this area, it is an important secondary area where numerous crops were developed and improved. Headed cabbages such as Milan cabbage, and sweet or Florence fennel (see above) are obvious examples. - Many beets, chicories, lettuces, kales and cauliflowers also came out of Italy, and broccoli was developed there as late as the 17th century.

Romanesco broccoli (see left) is a recently revived heritage variety from Northern Italy, where the head consists of spiralling pale green florets resembling a minaret.

BEETROOT

A great diversity of beetroot varieties exist, from the two-tone concentric red and white rings of Dolce di Chiogga, through many rich purple varieties to the golden skin and creamy yellow flesh of Golden Beet. The popularity of beetroot as a vegetable has suffered from its reputation as animal fodder, but many varieties are very delicately flavoured, and they can also be very decorative.

LEFT: *Chinese cabbage is hardy and easy to grow, providing valuable greens at times of the year when there are few other leafy vegetables available.*

Travelling the other way across the Atlantic, the early settlers of North America took with them seeds of numerous crops unavailable in the New World. Surprisingly, although the homelands of the potato were relatively close at hand in Central and South America, this crop too was first introduced to North America via Europe.

Much of America's more recent vegetable heritage reflects the history of the many different immigrant groups that have come there. The past 150 years have seen huge migrations of population, and the US now treasures a rich patchwork of family heirlooms from northern countries such as Russia and Sweden, down through Germany and the rest of Central Europe, to those coming from as far south as Italy. Ironically, these heirlooms have sometimes been more diligently maintained by immigrant communities than in their countries of origin.

Although we are long past the time when newly discovered continents reveal completely new staple crops, some vegetables have moved across the world in relatively recent times. Chinese cabbage, for example, recorded in China as early as the 5th century AD, did not reach America and Europe until the end of the 19th century – probably brought from the East by missionaries. The value of many Oriental vegetables has only been recognised by Western gardeners in the last 10 or 20 years. Yet many of these leafy vegetables are excellently adapted to cool temperate climates, and make excellent fall and early spring crops.

Unlike the tropical latitudes of the developing world, which contain a rich indigenous diversity of nearly all the major vegetables, the Northern developed countries have always been reliant on travellers – and we should not ignore them now. Like our ancestors, we should continue to explore the potential of plants from other parts of the world which could increase the diversity of our food crops, as well as adding to our medicinal knowledge, and enrich our vegetable heritage.

How crops developed

Wherever in the world they originated, all our crops initially developed from wild plants. Primitive people were hunter-gatherers, killing wild animals and fish, and collecting leaves, nuts, roots and berries for food. However, once groups started settling down in one place, they began to sow and tend some of the wild food plants and the domestication of crops began.

These early farmers knew nothing about genetics, but while working with their crops they would have spotted some plants that were better than others: those that grew more vigorously, or had larger and sweeter fruit, or thicker and more tender roots, for example. They would select these for saving seed, and the yields and qualities of the crop would gradually evolve, each generation improving upon the last. In the same way, undesirable characteristics such as prickles or bitterness were selected out. The farmers were in fact choosing plants with a more useful genetic make-up.

Sometimes natural crossing would occur between closely related species that were growing in the same field or in the field margins, producing plants that were quite different. In addition, sudden spontaneous internal changes would occasionally occur within plant cells, giving useful mutations or 'sports' of the plant. By selecting these natural hybrids and sports for seed saving, new variations were developed.

For most of our crops, this process of domestication has been continuing for hundreds, sometimes thousands of years, and they are far removed from their wild forms. Only a few crops, such as sea kale (*Crambe maritima*) and corn salad (*Valerianella locusta*), are still easily recognisable in their natural state. A plump Savoy cabbage, or a cauliflower with tight white curds, bear little resemblance to their ancestral wild cabbage, a straggly and unattractive creature. However, if you let some cultivated brassicas run to flower, they will reveal how similar they are to each other, and to the wild plants.

CULTIVATED CABBAGE

The earliest brassicas, directly descended from wild cabbage, were rather unattractive plants, with tough glaucous leaves running up a thick straggling stem.

Over centuries, the species developed to produce many varieties which are beautiful enough to grace any ornamental landscape, such as the finely veined and curled leaves of this Savoy cabbage in frost.

KALES

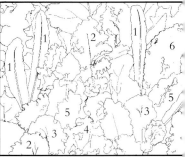

1. Lacinato

2. Russian Red

3. Halbhoher Moosbacher
   Winter Hellgrüner

4. Siberian

5. Krasnaya Kuroavafa
   Vysokaja

6. Niedriger Grüner
   Feinstekrause

TOMATOES IN ALL COLOURS, SHAPES AND SIZES

Some tomatoes – such as Red Currant, or Broad Ripple Yellow Currant – have fruits that are little more than the size of blackcurrants. They are best harvested by shaking the plant upside down. In contrast, the old beefsteak variety Big Rainbow (*see below*) can have fruit weighing three pounds (1.5kg) or more.

The colour of a tomato depends on both its skin colour and the colour of the flesh. A red-fleshed tomato with a translucent skin looks pink, and a tomato with a yellow flesh and translucent skin looks white. Some white tomatoes do have flesh that is also almost white. At the opposite colour extreme are the 'black' tomatoes, many of which were developed in Russia: Black Krim from the Black Sea, for example, has very dark brownish-purple skin and reddish-brown flesh. Yellow Pear, which dates from the late 1800s, is (as its name suggests) pear-shaped; others are bulbous and deeply ribbed such as the Mexican variety Zapotec (*see right*), believed to be the ancestor of all beefsteak-type tomatoes.

Their internal structure also varies – paste or processing tomatoes have a solid flesh, often described as meaty, with few seeds; stuffing tomatoes are almost hollow inside: the seeds

are clustered together in the centre and can be easily removed, making the fruit ideal for filling with savoury mixtures. One interesting lobed type, known by Central American Indians as a 'traveller tomato', consists of individual cavities so the fruit can be divided simply by tearing it apart – no picnic knife needed for these!

The most important characteristic of the tomato for gardeners is, of course, taste. The gel around the seeds significantly affects the flavour of the fruit, particularly its acidity, and how it feels in the mouth. The less acid the gel of a particular variety, the sweeter the fruit – although growing conditions also play a part, and most varieties are sweeter if grown in plenty of sunshine. Paste tomatoes with few seeds (and therefore little gel) are rather bland, without the taste or texture desirable in a salad tomato.

Adaptation to climate

As crops that are domesticated in one area move to a neighbouring area, where perhaps rainfall is higher, or frost more severe, or the soil heavier, they gradually adapt to the new conditions. In each generation, some plants survive the particular conditions better than others, and these – aided by farmer selection – contribute disproportionately more to the next generation. Differences in conditions between neighbouring areas are often subtle ones, but occasionally plants have had to adapt to more marked changes – as when crops used to the tropical conditions of South America were first brought to Europe, with its shorter growing seasons and longer days.

People in different regions may have different tastes and needs – preferring potatoes with denser tubers, for example, or with purple skins – and this has always influenced the way a crop has developed. A wide range of local crop types known as 'landraces' traditionally evolved in response to such different situations, each with distinct traits, but lacking the uniformity of today's highly bred vegetable varieties. Landraces are sometimes referred to as 'folk varieties', recognising the important role that rural communities have played (and still play), in developing and maintaining them.

As crops become adapted to climate and soil conditions, they also develop defences against local pests and diseases. When a pest or disease overcomes a particular defence mechanism within the plant, that crop will re-adapt, and so will the pest, and so on. Plants and their predators have always evolved alongside each other. Wide-ranging pest and disease resistance is an important feature of the old landraces.

THE POTATO IN EUROPE

The potato that came to Europe from South America in the 16th century did not produce the abundance of smooth round tubers that we expect to harvest from our plants today. The tubers were small and knobbly, the plants were susceptible to infection, and yields were low. It was grown initially as a garden curiosity rather than a serious crop – in England in 1716 it was considered much less important than the radish. This poor performance was not necessarily because of the change of climate, but because the life cycle of these potatoes was dependent on the short equatorial days in their homeland.

However, gradually the crop began to adapt to longer growing days – and by the mid 18th century potatoes were widely grown on a commercial basis, both for human and for animal consumption. Even in the Nordic countries, further still removed from the potato's tropical origins, varieties were developed which did well in the very long days and cool short growing seasons. Some of the old Nordic varieties still in existence today are particularly valued for their long dormancy times and resistance to certain storage diseases.

SWEET PEPPERS

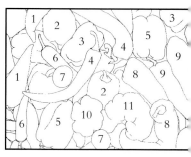

1. Pimento

2. Lorelei

3. Gold Star

4. Jimmý Nardello's

5. Ariane

6. Tequila Sunrise

7. Sweet Cherry

8. Early Prolific Banana

9. Sweet Melrose

10. Red Cheese Pimento

11. Quadrati D'Asti Giallo

Modern plant breeding

For millennia, farmers and gardeners were the plant breeders, improving crops by selection from generation to generation. In the 19th century, rather than waiting for changes to occur at random in nature, a few experimenters started to make deliberate crosses between plants. By choosing the plants carefully, these early hybridisers hoped that the offspring would have the desirable characteristics of both parents.

The Vilmorin-Andrieux family in France were pioneers in European plant breeding in the 19th century, as was Luther Burbank in the United States – who gained particular fame for his work with potatoes. However, it was only when the experimental work of the Austro-Silesian monk Gregor Mendel was recognised in the early 1900s that hybridisation gained a real scientific basis, and gave more predictable results. Prior to that, it had been largely a hit and miss affair.

At first new varieties were developed by individuals and small family-based seedsmen, still with the involvement of farmers and gardeners, but techniques gradually became more sophisticated. There were also pressures to make plants of the same variety less variable, so those with slightly 'wrong' characteristics (for commercial purposes) were weeded out. Over several generations varieties were developed that were very uniform and reproduced that uniformity, these were known as 'pure lines'. In the 1930s the first 'F1 hybrid' corn varieties were produced, the seed of which came from crossing two inbred pure lines. F1 hybrids of other crops soon followed.

In the last 25 years, plant breeding has become the specialist realm of microbiologists, geneticists and other scientists. It is a complex major industry. Dozens of potato varieties, for

LONG-KEEPING TOMATOES

A tomato that would stay fresh and firm on the supermarket shelf for weeks was the marketing dream that inspired the variety Flavr Savr. Genetic engineers spliced in genes to change the enzyme polygalacturonase, which naturally occurs in the fruits, so that they would decompose more slowly. As a result, it was said that the Flavr Savr tomato would stay in good condition for up to 50 days.

Yet many traditional tomato varieties already have very long shelf life. Before tomatoes could be imported out of season, they were deliberately selected so that they could be stored for several months and used in the winter. Garden Peach, for example is a heritage variety with excellent keeping qualities. Orange-pink fruit ripens very slowly off the vine, and stores well without loss of taste or texture. Traditional gardeners used to pick these in the autumn, and would still be eating them after Christmas.

example, can be screened for blight resistance in the glasshouse within 3-4 weeks of germination, rather than growing them in a field for several months, and any useful material resulting can be held in test tubes using tissue culture. Genetic engineering allows specific genes in plants to be located and marked in the laboratory, and then moved between species in a way that was never possible with traditional hybridisation methods.

Neither farmers nor gardeners are now critically involved in plant development. It is geared to the perceived needs of industry, which is typically concerned with relatively short-term gain. Plant breeding has also become extremely expensive, for example, the development and marketing of one of the first genetically engineered varieties to be released, the Flavr Savr tomato (*see facing page*), is said to have cost in excess of 95 million US dollars. With such invest-ment, it is no wonder that a few varieties dominate the shelves of superstores and the pages of catalogues.

THE EARLY DAYS

We have come a long way since the days when the Mayflower sailed from Plymouth in 1620, taking the Pilgrim Fathers to establish the first English colony in North America. Ever since then, seeds have been carried by migrants round the world. A ship sailing from England to North America in 1631 carried supplies of parsnip, beet, cabbage, carrot, cauliflower, leek, onion and radish seed, none of which would have then been obtainable across the Atlantic. The most expensive item then was two ounces of cauliflower seeds which cost five shillings (25p/35 cents).

F1 HYBRIDS AND OPEN-POLLINATED VARIETIES

The creation of an F1 hybrid first involves selecting two parent plants with desired characteristics and inbreeding them (not allowing them to exchange pollen with others) until two very pure, distinct, and uniform lines are produced. These lines are then married, all the pollen coming from one parent and all the egg cells from the other. The resulting seed is what you buy in an expensive packet of an F1 hybrid variety. It will give you progeny (the F1 or first filial generation) which all have the desirable traits from both parents, and which all exhibit 'hybrid vigour'. This means that they will usually outgrow and outyield plants of traditional open-pollinated varieties.

Unfortunately, the seeds of these F1 plants do not produce the same high class offspring, but a motley selection – and sometimes the seeds will not germinate at all. In contrast, the seeds of open-pollinated varieties will produce offspring that are true-to-type, although without the same strict unifor-mity as F1 hybrids.

❷
THE IMPORTANCE OF DIVERSITY

ABOVE: *Traditional in Italy, this majestic onion came to the US via David Cavagnaro's family.*

LEFT: *Scorzonera, celeriac and mooli radishes are as easy to grow as kohl rabi, beets, parsnips and common root vegetables.*

Now that vigorous F1 hybrids dominate the seed catalogues, and crops can be tailored to our needs by genetic engineering, it is tempting to think that the old varieties are redundant. It is true that new varieties do give high yields under the right conditions; they can have good resistance to specific pests and diseases; they make harvest times predictable, and they have made enormous and valuable contributions to the world's food-producing capacity. The danger is that they will cause us to abandon and neglect the broad genetic base of our traditional wild and cultivated plants.

Modern plant breeding on its own can never provide solutions to every question, and traditional open-pollinated varieties, landraces or folk varieties and their wild relatives will always have crucial roles to play. They have indispensable qualities and a diversity in their genetic make-up which cannot be replaced.

It was lack of such diversity early in plant-breeding history that led to the Irish potato famine of 1845. After the potato was introduced into Europe from South America in the 16th century, it took time to adapt to northern conditions, but by the 1840s it was widely grown, and had become a staple food in Ireland. In the autumn of 1845, the potatoes there were struck by a devastating and previously unknown fungal disease – so virulent that some correspondents at the time labelled it 'cholera', but we now identify it as late blight. Any gardener who has experienced this disease will know just how quickly it spreads through potato foliage, and will recognise the unmistakable stench it creates as the tubers rot.

One million people died in Ireland in 1845; another million emigrated. In many areas farmers lost 90% of their tubers and it took a decade for the situation to recover. This epidemic happened because all the varieties of potato growing in Europe at that time were derived from just two parent varieties, the two brought from the Andes that had adapted most successfully to the northern climate. They produced reliable yields in the cool wet conditions of Northern Europe, but Andean potatoes had never encountered blight and so had no resistance to it. Once the disease got a hold on one plant, there was nothing to stop it spreading quickly to attack all the rest.

Such epidemics of monoculture have happened on many occasions since, destroying crops of wheat, corn and rice in different areas of the world (*see pages 41 and 48*).

Past, present and future

In the 1850s, after the potato famine years, growers in Europe realised the importance of using a wider spread of parent varieties for breeding. They imported more varieties from America to develop the crop and widen its genetic characteristics. However, it was not until the 20th century, when scientific expeditions collected wild potatoes from Central and South America, that European varieties with significant resistance to blight began to be developed. In the 1950s and early 1960s, several potatoes containing resistance genes from the Mexican species *Solanum demissum* were bred in the UK. High resistance to blight has also recently been found in other Mexican species such as *Solanum papita* and *Solanum polydenum*.

Scientists working on the development of other major crops are also using landraces and wild ancestors of vegetables from the centres of diversity. Until very recently, most commercially grown varieties of soya beans in the US were derived from a handful of imported lines; their narrow genetic base made them vulnerable to epidemics. Now seed from 500 different soya bean strains has been brought to the US from Central China, where the bean originated, and these are being used in current breeding programmes. One of the problems they may help to solve is that of *phytophthora* root rot – a major fungal disease of soya beans, which can kill seedlings and reduce yields of older plants, particularly on poorly drained soils. Not surprisingly, resistance to this disease has been found predominantly in soya bean lines from rainy wet areas of Central China.

Similarly, wild lettuces such as *Lactuca serriola* are being used to breed resistance against downy mildew into modern iceberg lettuce, and hybridisation of the cultivated tomato *Lycopersicon esculentum* with wild species such as *L. pimpinellifolium* has been used to confer pest and disease resistance on many of the new varieties on the market today.

Traditional varieties, selected by farmers and gardeners over many years and generations of cultivation, are more closely related to modern ones, but these old varieties can also be important to plant breeders. Developed because of their reliability and adaptability, they are more likely to thrive without additional chemical fertilisers, pesticides or irrigation than their modern counterparts. Some of them will also have good storage qualities dating back to the days before the widespread use of refrigeration and controlled atmosphere stores. These are just the sort of characteristics that could be valuable in years to come.

No one really knows what the future holds, no matter how many predictions scientists come up with. Global warming may give many places more extreme conditions – hotter summers, harder frosts, extended droughts. Less ozone in the atmosphere is already causing an increase in ultra-violet rays, and who knows what pests and diseases might arise in 10, 50 or 100 years' time? We can only guess at the long-term effects on plants. Modern plant breeders may be able to create new varieties with some of the required traits, but they can only do so by making use of existing ones – they cannot create new genes.

Many characteristics of our wild crops and old varieties are as yet unnoticed, unvalued, unrecognised or unneeded. These qualities may be vitally important in the future. By preserving as diverse a range of plants as possible, we will have the greatest chance of adapting future varieties as the situation demands. Otherwise we are putting the security of all our future food supplies in jeopardy.

Recycled genes
....

Through scientific and technological advances we now know how to use wild crop species and old landraces in plant breeding, but this rarely offers successful simple solutions.

You only have to look at the difference between a tall spindly wild lettuce and a large-hearted iceberg to see the difficulties involved in using the wild form as a parent. Similarly, wild tomatoes may have extremely desirable qualities of disease resistance, but they also have many less attractive characteristics such as tiny fruits and rampant growth. Breeding the good qualities into a modern crop, whilst eliminating the undesirable ones, takes long and expensive breeding programmes.

Plant breeders are much more likely to get reliable results quickly, and cheaply, if they work from closely related plants. So commercial pressures to save time and money mean that many modern varieties are simply re-mixtures of each other. There is little true variation in their genetic make-up, and within each variety the plants are extremely uniform. This means that even when some new genetic material has been introduced into a crop, the beneficial results may be limited.

If disease resistance is conferred on a variety by one major gene, and this variety or a similar one is planted over a large area, the resistance will soon break down. The greater the continuous area of similar varieties that the disease encounters, the greater will be the pressure on it to adapt and spread. This is what happened to the first blight-resistant potatoes that were developed containing a simple type of resistance using genes from the wild species *Solanum demissum*. The blight fungus soon adapted and evolved strains which made this type of resistance almost useless.

A disastrous outbreak of the fungal disease Southern leaf blight in America's corn crop in 1970 illustrates the problem caused by plant breeders 'recycling' genes. Since the 1950s, most corn grown commercially in the US had consisted of hybrid varieties bred using material from one male sterile variety, giving plants tassels with impotent pollen. This prevented self-pollination and made the process of hybridisation much easier and cheaper. Up till then the tassels had had to be removed by hand.

Unfortunately this same common feature made all the varieties susceptible to leaf blight. In the summer of 1970, this disease ruined the corn crop. In the Southern States many farmers lost their entire crop, and in the US as a whole, 15% of the crop was lost.

Despite this warning, nearly all commercial corn – both that for grinding into cornmeal or flour and that for sweetcorn – now consists of just a few genetically similar hybrid varieties. Compare this to the two or three hundred local landraces of corn that the Native Americans were growing when the first Europeans arrived – corns with amazingly wide genetic diversity. They varied in the colour and form of the grain, and were tailored to the local environment, and their end use (*see page 56*). They were tended on numerous small plots – a far cry from the monocultures found today. The first European settlers adopted these various local varieties, and it was not until the mid 1800s that the emphasis began to be placed on larger more uniform ears and much of the diversity was lost. Then in the 1930s the first hybrid corns were produced.

Some primitive corns are still available through specialist seed suppliers in the US concerned with protecting and maintaining endangered plants, and a few traditional farmers also still maintain commercial varieties of open-pollinated corn.

POTATOES

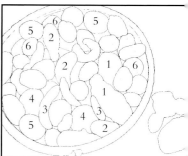

1. Siberian
2. Purple Peruvian
3. German Finger
4. Ashworth
5. Red Erik
6. Caribe

Protection through diversity

One of the best ways to combat the effects of a pest or disease outbreak is to plant mixed crops, using traditional varieties with more variable characteristics. Even where a disease may find it easy to overcome one plant, it will probably struggle to make inroads to the next few. Their leaf surfaces might be less easily penetrated, for example, or the fungus might not be able to spread quickly through their tissues. Usually a combination of factors is responsible for the resistance, and because some plants are vulnerable, there is not the same pressure on the disease to overcome it. Even though the overall yield of such a mixed crop will never be as high as that of a single immune variety, it will never run the risk of being devastated by an epidemic.

It is difficult to get such lasting resistance in a single modern variety. It usually means working with many different genes and poses a considerable challenge to the plant breeder. Even then other unexpected problems may occur. Just as plants of uniform modern varieties can have the same susceptibility to an unexpected pest or disease, so will they all have the same reaction to any other kind of environmental change. Only by maintaining a wide genetic base will plants have the chance to survive in the future.

Traditional methods of gardening and farming are not only important for maintaining old varieties as an essential raw material for plant breeding, they also encapsulate a whole world of valuable information about selection, propagation, seed saving, cultivation and use of the crop. The traditional ways of growing crops often illustrate the best ways of protecting diversity. This knowledge must not be allowed to die out.

RESPONSES TO DISEASE

Late blight, the fungus behind the Irish potato famine, originates in Mexico, where most varieties have therefore developed some type of resistance. However, the disease evolves to try and overcome resistance, so every year some strain of blight attacks Mexican potato crops.

To minimise the effect of these attacks, Mexican farmers plant up to 30 varieties in a single field. They cannot predict where the blight will strike, and recognise that some variety, or varieties, will inevitably succumb. But the others will survive and flourish, so the farmers will always have a potato harvest even if parts of the crop fail. Their entire crop will never be devastated.

The response in more 'developed' agricultural systems is different. A few varieties are planted over large areas, so the blight fungus quickly overcomes any inbred resistance that they have. To prevent epidemics, the potato growers must therefore spray their crops routinely with fungicides. The plant breeders breed new 'resistant' varieties, but the high cost of the breeding programmes dictates that they must sell a few varieties widely to recoup the cost – so these few varieties are planted over a large area… and the problem carries on.

LUMPERS POTATO

A late maincrop variety giving excellent yields of large knobbly tubers, Lumpers was the mainstay of Irish potato plantings at the time of the 1845 famine. It was highly susceptible if blight struck in July before the tubers had bulked up.

Outside Ireland the variety was said to have poor flavour and little culinary merit. But when museum stocks were grown out in 1995, marking the 150th anniversary of the famine, many people remarked how good it was to eat – probably compared to most varieties which are commercially grown today.

LETTUCE BREEDING FOR DOWNY MILDEW RESISTANCE

A high proportion of all fungicide applications to commercial varieties of lettuce in Northern Europe are administered in the attempt to control downy mildew. This disease has developed races which have overcome nearly all current resistance in commercial lettuce varieties. Breeding for resistance is an important part of a 20-year lettuce breeding programme in the UK at Horticultural Research International (HRI). Scientists there are using four wild lettuce varieties – *Lactuca serriola*, *L. virosa*, *L. aculeata* and *L. salinga* – as the primary sources of new resistance genes.

The biggest problem in the programme has been to obtain a lettuce that has both resistance and acceptable quality, as the wild lettuce are far removed from consumers' ideas of what constitutes an acceptable lettuce. Whereas the marketplace wants crisp-leaved and tight-hearted lettuces, wild varieties tend to be long stemmed and straggly, with uneven leaf growth. It has taken two decades to produce iceberg varieties containing one of the new resistant genes, now being trialled by commercial growers.

These varieties are successful at present, but it is only a matter of time before new races of downy mildew will evolve to overcome their resistance. So HRI scientists are also looking at ways of using the old variety Iceberg, or Batavia Blonde. This lettuce has good resistance to downy mildew, resistance that seems to have lasted since at least the middle of the last century without threat from evolved races of the disease.

Still grown by gardeners today, Batavia Blonde appeared in a seed list from the Vilmorin seed company in 1856. Although it is not actually immune to downy mildew, the disease does not spread through a whole crop in the way that it affects other varieties – fewer plants are infected, and the symptoms of the infected plants are less severe.

The reason that this old lettuce variety is not attacked in the same way as others is due to the complex genetics of the resistance – probably involving at least six genes. This makes the effect much stronger than if it were conferred by one single gene; however the complexity also makes the resistance much more difficult for scientists to isolate.

LETTUCES

LEFT: Reine des Glaces is a tight headed gourmet lettuce from France. Its lace-fringed leaves are deeply cut, pointed and lace-fringed, adding a special touch to any salad.

BELOW (TOP): The light yellow-green leaves of Australian Yellow are very tender and slightly sweet; this variety is excellent for hot climates as it does not bolt easily.

BELOW (BOTTOM): Although Bronze Arrow is a heritage variety from California it is also very hardy and adaptable, suitable for most climates. The large leaves are shaped like arrowheads, green with a reddish bronze tinge.

High-yielding varieties

The overriding factor which determines whether a new variety is judged successful is yield. Even when plant breeders are looking for other characteristics such as disease resistance, only varieties whose yields are at least as good as their rivals are likely to be considered for development. However, yield is typically measured on monitored test sites with high inputs of chemical fertilisers and pesticides, and with optimum irrigation.

Modern varieties perform well in such ideal conditions, but can fail dramatically when they are less favourable. This has had most obviously disastrous results for farmers in developing countries swept up in the so-called 'Green Revolution'. In the late 1960s high-yield varieties of wheat and rice were developed, mainly in American and Japanese breeding programmes. These new varieties responded well to applications of nitrogen fertiliser, and initially had some resistance to major pests and diseases. They were soon replacing traditional varieties used by peasant farmers, who were promised reliable plants with amazingly high yields, despite poor conditions.

At first initial production was greatly increased. However, the pests and diseases quickly adapted, and the new strains began to need not only fertilisers, but pesticides and fungicides. They also needed herbicides, because the high levels of fertiliser promoted weed growth, and machinery to apply these sprays. Irrigation schemes were also essential. Seeds of the new strains were in many cases initially too expensive for subsistence farmers to purchase, and they became dependent on additional costly inputs – without them, the new varieties were often less productive than the old ones. One of the causes of the Ethiopian famine

in the 1980s was the fact that the country had abandoned its traditional drought-tolerant crops and varieties in favour of new ones.

Around the same time, another problem with high yield varieties occurred in the Philippines, when a 'miracle' hybrid strain of rice was hit by disease, destroying whole crops. Rice growers switched to another hybrid form, which proved vulnerable to other diseases and pests; so farmers moved on to yet another hybrid that was resistant to almost all local diseases and pests, but vulnerable to wind. When breeders eventually decided to return to a traditional strain that had grown well in harsh weather, they found this strain was now almost unavailable as indigenous farmers had planted all their rice fields with the 'miracle' hybrids.

Yet another disadvantage of the new varieties has been their failure to fit in with local farming systems. For example, hybrid varieties of wheat had short stems which did not provide straw for feeding animals or thatching roofs. Moreover, many of the farmers who for centuries had saved seed of their traditional varieties for the next year's crop, found that this was no longer possible. Either the varieties were hybrids, so saved seed failed to give a good crop in the second and subsequent years, or their disease resistance had broken down to the point where they needed to be replaced with the latest (temporarily) less susceptible strains.

Although the consequences are, in the short term, nowhere near so far-reaching, the same problem applies to modern vegetable varieties grown by gardeners and small organic growers – particularly on marginal land or in difficult climates. The conditions under which new varieties are developed are often very different to those in your backgarden, and traditional varieties – particularly those of local origin – will probably outperform the new ones.

Gardeners' needs

Traditional varieties have other qualities that make them more useful to gardeners and small growers than their modern counterparts. Modern varieties of many vegetables, such as peas and corn, are bred to mature all at once so that they can be harvested by machine, and new brassica and lettuce varieties will all head simultaneously to satisfy the commercial market. Home gardeners do not want such gluts and famines. Beware of catalogue descriptions that say a variety is 'good for freezing' – this usually means that it will need harvesting all at once. Traditional varieties – tall peas, old types of lettuce, open-pollinated sweetcorn, cabbage and cauliflower – are more likely to crop over a long period.

Processors and supermarkets want uniform crops – carrots the same length, parsnips the same shape, cauliflowers the same size – so that they can be packed and priced by machine. They are also looking for resistance to bruising, so that vegetables are not damaged by being sorted on a conveyor belt, or by travelling long distances from the grower to a centralised packing house and back out again. It has been said that new hybrid tomatoes destined for the US supermarket trade are tested in the same Florida laboratory that tests car bumpers!

Gardeners, however, like to harvest according to the recipe and the occasion, and variation in the size of vegetables can be a positive advantage. Produce only has to survive a trip up the garden path; far from wanting tomatoes with tough skins, they want fruit that dissolves in the mouth or on cooking - as many traditional varieties do.

What gardeners want above all is taste, yet this seems rarely considered as a priority in modern vegetable breeding programmes. It is a quality that is mentioned again and again in descriptions of old varieties, whether they are leafy crops, roots or fruits. Of course, even a standard hybrid variety does taste better grown at home and gathered fresh rather than picked from a supermarket, but the sweet perfumed taste of, for example, some of the heritage melons, such as the 19th century French Noir des Carmes, or the British Blenheim Orange is unsurpassed. The cantaloupe variety Old Time Tennessee is said to be so fragrant that you can find the melons in the dark!

OPEN-POLLINATED SWEETCORN

Most sweetcorn varieties sold to gardeners are now F1 hybrids. Their cobs are uniform in size, and tend to mature all at once – only an advantage if you want to freeze them. The newest hybrid corns contain special genes to make them 'supersweet'; they are very sugary and hold their sweetness for some time after they have been picked – a useful attribute for supermarket sales, but quite unnecessary for home gardeners. Moreover, these varieties can be difficult to germinate in less than ideal conditions, and seedlings often lack vigour.

Many gardeners still prefer the taste of the traditional open-pollinated sweetcorns such as Golden Bantam. This was introduced by the pioneering American plant breeder Burpee in 1902 and until recently was widely available both in the US and Europe. However, even this old favourite variety has recently been dropped from the lists of major commercial companies.

RAINBOW CHARD

Some strikingly attractive varieties, now fashionable for their decorative qualities in modern potagers and edible landscapes, are in fact of very ancient origin.

A red chard, ancestor of the widely grown Rhubarb or Ruby chard, which has bright red leaf stalks, was described by Aristotle in the 4th century. Vilmorin, in *The Vegetable Garden* (1885) lists Chilian Beet, or Red-stalked Swiss chard, grown for a table vegetable but also as an ornamental plant. A yellow form is also mentioned in the book.

This Rainbow chard is a spectacular mixture of the vivid colours which have been found in old varieties.

Links with the past

Traditional varieties are not only of practical value for present and future gardeners, they also provide inextricable links to local history and local culture; to major historical events, and to other people in other times.

The potato, Lumpers, for example (*see page 45*), provides a direct historical link to the Irish potato famine, illustrating the potential disasters inherent in lack of diversity. Other varieties have purely local relevance. Particular agriculture practices have historically affected the pattern of work and the nature of the landscape. Local businesses such as that of the French 'Onion Johnnies' selling Brittany's Roscoff onions, developed on the strength of certain crops (*see page 57*). Local festivals and customs associated with particular varieties exist all over the world, such as the tradition, in North East England, of eating Carlin peas on 'Carlin Sunday' (*see right*).

Religious significance has sometimes become attached to certain varieties. Many of the diverse coloured corns of Native American tribes were used for sacred rituals, and spiritual significance has also been attributed to the fascinatingly beautiful markings and forms of bean seeds. The large number of old landraces of drying peas in Sweden is said to be due to their pre-Christian tradition of eating pea soup on Thursdays – the Swedish people were said to believe that peas were the food of their god Thor, and Thursday was 'Thor's day'.

To immigrant families in any country, seeds brought from their homelands were not only important to maintain their diet but to keep alive a link with their roots - even more so when emigration had been by necessity rather than choice. The Cherokee Indians Trail of Tears bean (*see opposite page*) came to symbolise their struggle against hard times.

CARLIN PEAS

Carlin peas are drying peas dating back to 16th century England; traditionally eaten in the North East of the country on 'Carlin Sunday', the fifth Sunday in Lent, two weeks before Easter.

The tradition is said to commemorate the relief of the famine that occurred in the area when it was besieged in 1644. Famine ended when a shipwreck threw up a cargo of Carlin peas, retrieved by the hungry people.

Carlins are small black peas with a slight mottle. The night before Carlin Sunday they are steeped in water, and the next day they are boiled, often with a ham bone or bacon fat, until they are soft and mushy.

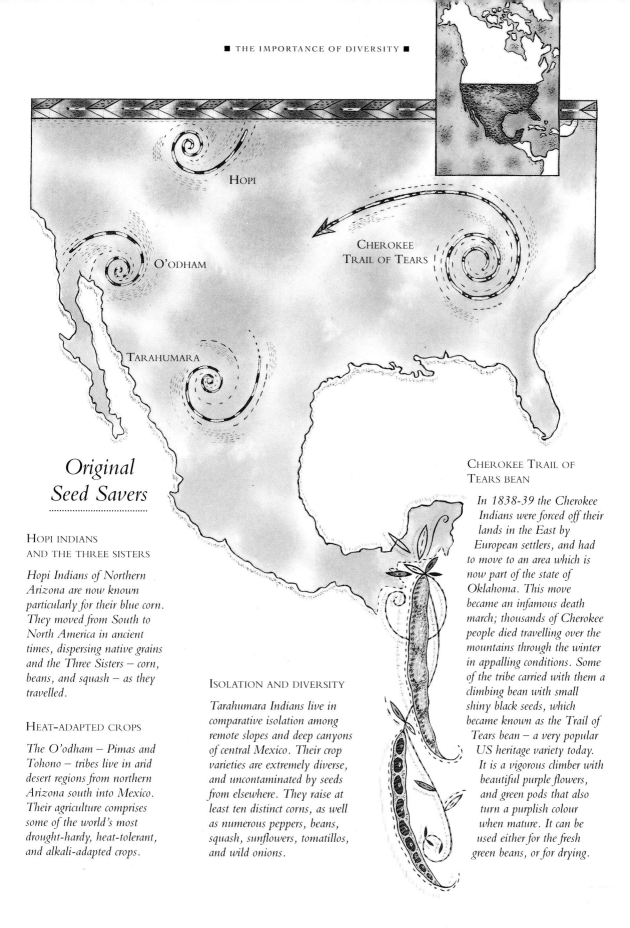

Original Seed Savers

HOPI INDIANS AND THE THREE SISTERS

Hopi Indians of Northern Arizona are now known particularly for their blue corn. They moved from South to North America in ancient times, dispersing native grains and the Three Sisters – corn, beans, and squash – as they travelled.

HEAT-ADAPTED CROPS

The O'odham – Pimas and Tohono – tribes live in arid desert regions from northern Arizona south into Mexico. Their agriculture comprises some of the world's most drought-hardy, heat-tolerant, and alkali-adapted crops.

ISOLATION AND DIVERSITY

Tarahumara Indians live in comparative isolation among remote slopes and deep canyons of central Mexico. Their crop varieties are extremely diverse, and uncontaminated by seeds from elsewhere. They raise at least ten distinct corns, as well as numerous peppers, beans, squash, sunflowers, tomatillos, and wild onions.

CHEROKEE TRAIL OF TEARS BEAN

In 1838-39 the Cherokee Indians were forced off their lands in the East by European settlers, and had to move to an area which is now part of the state of Oklahoma. This move became an infamous death march; thousands of Cherokee people died travelling over the mountains through the winter in appalling conditions. Some of the tribe carried with them a climbing bean with small shiny black seeds, which became known as the Trail of Tears bean – a very popular US heritage variety today. It is a vigorous climber with beautiful purple flowers, and green pods that also turn a purplish colour when mature. It can be used either for the fresh green beans, or for drying.

HOPI

O'ODHAM

TARAHUMARA

CHEROKEE TRAIL OF TEARS

CORNS

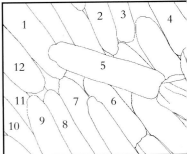

1. Reid's Yellow

2. Rainbow Dent

3. Mandan Red Flour

4. Strubbe's Calico

5. Northwest Red Dent

6. Strubbe's Purple

7. Northern Bloody Butcher

8. Hickory King

9. Blue Clarage

10. Purple Husk Cob

11. Narragousett

12. Southern Bloody Butcher

NATIVE AMERICAN CORNS

The Native American word for corn 'mahiz', means 'our life'. Corn is their prime food of life, it is also vital in many sacred rituals. They traditionally culture six colours of corn: black, red, white, yellow, blue and multicoloured. Each colour represents one of the Six Directions – north, east, south, west, zenith (Father Sky) and nadir (Mother Earth). In different areas, different colours have become specialities, in response to growing conditions and particular preferences. For example Northeastern Indians use white corn for breads, while blue corn is the choice of the Southwestern Indians.

Atlantic Coast Indians provided the first settlers with corn, and taught them how to pound or grind it for bread. These early settlers went on to develop their own colours and varieties. Sweetcorn developed comparatively recently, created by natural mutations from flint or dent corn around the middle of the 18th century.

Southwestern Indian corns have evolved in close association with beneficial soil fungi, mycorrhizae – which make the roots 10 times more efficient in extracting soil nutrients. These fungi cease to function at high chemical fertiliser levels. Some of the old Native American corn fields are over 800 years old; they have never been fertilised, the fertility has been maintained by mycorrhizae and through inter-planting with beans.

PEAS BEFORE THE FREEZER

Peas for drying have been grown since ancient times, but peas used fresh from the pod did not become popular until the 16th century when new strains were developed by Italian gardeners. These first shelling peas had smooth round seeds and were very hardy. Their descendants are still used by gardeners today to make early and overwintering sowings, extending the harvest of fresh peas. One of the oldest round seeded peas still grown, Prince Albert, was probably introduced around 1840, the year Albert married Queen Victoria. Sown in January, it can produce a crop of peas in May, and if some of these are saved and sown in July, they will crop in September.

In the 18th century came different strains of sweeter but less hardy peas, easily distinguished by their seeds which have a wrinkled appearance. The first varieties of these sweet podding peas were very tall, growing to 2m (6ft 6in) or more, and cropped over a long period.

When these varieties were first grown on a field scale, they had to be picked and podded by hand. In the early 1900s, children in the main pea-growing areas of England were allowed six weeks holiday from school during the pea harvest so that they could help with picking, and the pods were subsequently shelled and graded by gangs of women at Covent Garden Market in London.

It was not until much later in the 20th century that the modern dwarf peas were developed, tailored to mechanical harvesting and the deep-freeze market. The plants of these varieties are often less than a metre (3 ft) tall with a deliberately shortened flowering period so that the pods are nearly all ready at exactly the same time. Conveniently for the harvester, the peas are mostly borne at the top of the plants, and (for added convenience) many of these varieties have few leaves.

These qualities are not generally useful to gardeners, and it is well worth seeking out some of the tall garden pea varieties that are still in cultivation such as Ne Plus Ultra (introduced in 1847), and Champion of England (1843). These varieties crop over a long period and have good overall yields. They can also be very ornamental: when the tall pea Magnum Bonum with its beautiful white flowers was displayed at the Chelsea Flower Show in London in 1992, many of the visitors mistook it for a sweet pea. Some other tall peas have lemon yellow or dark purple pods, some of them are delicious fresh, others are particularly good for soups and some are best dried.

Vegetable names and histories

The names of old vegetable varieties often link them with people, places, or history, and hint at a story to be told. In the US, vegetables are often connected with people, and heirloom varieties such as Grandpa Admires lettuce (*see page 20*), Bill Jump's soup pea, or Boothby's Blond cucumber (*see page 17*), indicate how varieties have been handed down though generations of one family. Many ancient varieties are named for their original breeders – Aztec Red Kidney, or Montezuma's Red beans – while the importance of Native American seed-savers is remembered in varieties such as Mandan Bride corn, or Hopi Black beans.

Many varieties went to the US with waves of immigrants, and you need only look at any page of a seed catalogue to find names of seeds which reflect their country of origin – Irish Cobbler and Swedish Peanut Fingerling potatoes, Old German and Costuloto Genovese tomatoes, and hundreds of others.

In Northern Europe, the market garden regions which supplied vegetables to the expanding industrial cities of the 18th and 19th centuries were particularly significant in the development of vegetable varieties. These areas produced countless distinct local strains. The Vale of Evesham (serving industrial towns in the English Midlands) gave its name to numerous varieties such as the Evesham Special Brussels sprout, while market garden areas serving Paris produced hundreds of locally recorded varieties – De Viroflay spinach, Milan de Pontoise cabbage and the onion Paille des Vertus are still popular today.

Other names tie in with folklore, like the Turkey Craw bean, a productive climbing snap bean grown by seed savers in the US, the original seed of which is said to have come from the craw of a turkey brought home by a hunter!

L'OIGNON DE ROSCOFF

Legend says that the pink Roscoff onion was brought to Brittany from Portugal by a local man from the town of Roscoff, who travelled along the West European coasts with Breton boats in the 16th century. The variety adapted well to the local weather and soil conditions in this corner of France, and flourished in a way that other onions have never done. It became very important to the local growers and the local diet.

In the mid 19th century, one farmer tried taking some onions across the Channel to sell in England and Wales – and such was his success that many others followed. By the end of the century there were 2000 of the French 'Onion Johnnies', traditionally dressed in blue and white striped jerseys and black berets, riding round the UK on bicycles festooned with onions. Up to the second world war, the Roscoff area still produced up to 50,000 tonnes of the special pink onions a year, each grower having his own strain and saving his own seed.

Roscoff onions are very mild and sweet, good in salads and salsas. They also store well. Although production is much less today, the variety is still grown commercially in Brittany, and there are still some Onion Johnnies travelling the UK – although times have changed and most have exchanged their traditional bicycles for smart vans!

3
PRESSURES FOR UNIFORMITY

ABOVE: *Traditional varieties of peas, like these snow peas, usually grow at least 6 feet tall, with peas at all heights.*

LEFT: *Round headed cabbage varieties such as the old European Dittmarshcer Früher store well without losing flavour.*

Despite the importance of traditional vegetable varieties, landraces and their wild ancestors, they are fast disappearing. Numerous inter-related factors are conspiring to force old varieties out and replace them with new ones. Pressures supporting this trend towards uniform modern vari-eties arise from the dominance of multinational companies in the seed trade, modern farming methods, industrial develop-ment with its related social pressures, and from the legislation governing the sales of seeds.

The statistics showing the extent of losses are frightening. In the US and Canada, two-thirds of the nearly 5000 non-hybrid vegetable varieties that were offered in 1984 catalogues had been dropped by 1994. The situation is even worse in Europe, where substantial num-bers of traditional varieties – often those adapted to local climates and cultures – which were available up to two decades ago can no longer be obtained. For example, in France the 1925 seed list of the Vilmorin seed company offered more varieties of cabbages, beetroot, melons and onions, than were available on the entire French seed market in the 1980s.

Gardeners do not need to read these figures to be convinced. Each year they find that yet more of their favourite varieties have disappeared from the seed catalogues, and have been replaced by new hybrids. Even where traditional open-pollinated varieties are still offered on the market, their existence is fragile since many of them are available from just one supplier. In 1994, up to 50% of all open-pollinated vegetable varieties (in the UK, the US and Canada) were such 'one source' varieties. If such a supply dries up, the variety is gone for ever.

For some vegetable species, the influx of new varieties has had particularly drastic consequences. For example, by the mid 1970s hybrids had replaced almost all the open-pollinated Brussels sprouts used by commercial producers in Europe, and the same was soon true of cabbages and cauliflowers. The danger to traditional varieties of these crops is compound-ed by the fact that, rather than raising them from seed, many gardeners buy brassica plants from garden centres or other stores, who in turn get them from commercial sources. So garden-ers end up with the same few modern varieties as the main growers. Brassica seed is one of the most difficult types for small seed companies to maintain in production, because the plants occupy space over a long period and readily

COTTAGER'S KALE

Few old Brassica varieties can compete with modern hybrids developed by the large seed corporations.

Cottager's Kale is an old English variety of kale, raised in the 1850s. It was described in a contemporary gardening manual as "...4 foot high when fully grown, clothed to the ground with immense rosette-like shoots of a bluish-green tint, which, when boiled, become a delicate green." It was easy to grow, and very hardy and productive, giving a useful harvest of young shoots in the spring months. Many growers considered it tender and fine flavoured.

In the early 1990s EW King, the company who produced the seed in the UK, decided that not enough was being sold for it to pay its way.

To generate a commercially viable quantity of new seed, plants of Cottager's Kale (a biennial) would have to occupy 1 acre of the company's land for two years. Also, kales cross-pollinate with each other, as well as with cabbages, cauliflowers, and Brussels sprouts. To keep the varieties pure on a commercial scale, they have to be grown at least a kilometre apart. A seed supplier such as Kings can only grow a limited number of Brassica for seed each year – so preference must be given to the best selling varieties.

Fortunately some dedicated individuals and seed saving organisations are continuing to grow Cottager's Kale; it is no longer available through any major commercial supplier.

cross-pollinate, so distinct varieties have to be grown in isolated cages, or separated from other varieties by substantial distances.

Now F1 hybrids are available for more crops than ever before. Nearly all corn in the US is from hybrid seed; almost all commercial growers in Europe use hybrid parsnips, for example, and the latest seed catalogues now even have new F1 hybrids of leeks and purple sprouting broccoli. The traditional varieties represent years of selection from growers and seedsmen, and as they disappear many valuable characteristics are undoubtedly lost.

This loss of cultivated vegetable varieties is tragic, but the genetic diversity represented by cultivated food crops in Northern Europe and the US is relatively small compared to the huge diversity of landraces, and the wild ancestors of crops in all the major centres of diversity. The dramatic extinction of so many of these – in Central and South America, through Africa, India, China, to Eastern and Southern Europe – is potentially catastrophic.

Many indigenous farmers have been encouraged to abandon their local strains of crops in favour of a few modern varieties, developed hundreds or thousands of miles away. These new varieties can be found in places as far afield as isolated Himalayan valleys, rural communities in Northern Russia, and in remote areas of the smallest African states. Even where the old varieties are still grown, they are often side-by-side with modern ones, so there is serious danger of cross-pollination occurring and contaminating the home-saved seed. In the Solomon Islands, for example, fine local varieties of small yellow watermelons, grown for generations by the subsistence farmers, have crossed with a larger imported hybrid variety; similarly local purple maize has crossed with a commonly grown white sweetcorn.

The rise of the multinationals

The seed trade has only relatively recently passed out of common experience into the hands of experts. Even 50 years ago farmers and gardeners routinely saved their own seed, and did amateur selection work to improve their own stocks. Their varieties were often taken up by small family-based seed firms, who also did their own plant breeding, and this work was complemented by public research institutes and universities. But in the 1960s this began to change, largely because of increasing sophistication in plant breeding techniques, and the rising use of oil-based chemicals in agriculture. Large multinational companies with primary interests in oil, chemicals and drugs, began to invest in the seed industry, and many small firms without the same resources could not compete. Those that were not bought out were lost – and their seed lists, containing many unique varieties, often vanished.

Throughout the 1970s and 1980s, the seed industry was in turmoil. In the US and Canada, from 1984 to 1987 more than 60 companies went out of business, or were taken over. The scene in Europe was similar. Until the 1960s Austria was a major seed-producing country, with many small breeders each producing varieties adapted to the country's different climatic areas. Now there is only one main commercial seed company, and 95% of the vegetable varieties sold in Austria are imported. In the West, more than 500 family seed firms were bought out completely in the two decades between 1970 and 1990. Familiar company names may remain on the seed packets, but their owners are often the big multinationals.

As such companies have come to dominate the marketplace, so they have also become increasingly involved in research and development into plant breeding. It became US government policy during the 1980s to phase out federal research into plant breeding in areas where private companies could compete. In Europe, breeding work similarly shifted out of public hands.

The varieties that interest the multinational companies most are the new hybrids, bred to grow commercially in the widest range of climates and conditions, assuring highest sales. Many of the most significant losses are those varieties specifically adapted to local conditions – a large international company is unlikely to be interested in the low-volume regional specialities that were once the staples of the small seed companies they bought out. Varieties suited only to marginal areas, or to home gardeners, are the first to be dropped.

The chemical fertilisers or pesticides needed for the new varieties are often supplied by the same businesses that supply the seeds, a co-dependency which does not encourage the breeding of naturally vigorous pest and disease-resistant varieties. The links to chemicals are sometimes quite direct: among an increasing number of examples is the soya bean variety created by the chemical giant, Monsanto, which has been genetically engineered to tolerate their own glyphosate herbicide (*Round-up*).

For large companies motivated solely by profit, it makes sense to concentrate on new hybrid varieties rather than traditional open-pollinated varieties; the seed from F1 hybrids will not come true to type, so farmers and gardeners cannot easily bypass the seed company by saving seed from their own crops. Even more significantly, newly developed (as well as newly '(re)discovered') varieties can bring companies extra revenue through the registration of plant patents, and the application of plant breeders' rights.

ITALIAN VEGETABLES

Many attractive heritage vegetables come from Italy, where traditional ways of cultivating and cooking vegetables have continued remarkably unchanged for centuries.

Italian emigrants have spread numerous well-known varieties far and wide across the globe. All broccoli varieties originally hail from Italy, as well as some leafy greens. A great diversity of beans, peppers, tomatoes and aubergines have been cultivated for many centuries in the warm Mediterranean climate, as well as the onions and garlic so vital to Italian cuisine.

Ownership of genetic resources

In the past our vegetable heritage and the knowledge associated with it was regarded as a common resource. In the early 1960s, however, a number of industrial countries agreed on the concept of plant breeders' rights (PBR), by which a breeder could officially register a new vegetable variety and then receive a royalty from all those that use it.

The intention of this legislation was to reward plant breeders for their work, and to stimulate new research. Varieties protected by PBR could still be used without obligation by breeders to develop new ones, and farmers had the right to save seed from them for their own use. Unfortunately, the trend since then has been for increasingly restrictive controls on plant varieties.

The World Trade Organisation now requires that Member States protect plant varieties by patents, or by an effective equivalent designed to fit the country's needs. The effects of patents are far-reaching: when plant genetic material is patented, the patent holder has sole rights over the material and every plant containing it. Under patent law, farmers and growers saving seed are liable to pay royalties on that seed. Similar restrictions apply to its use for plant breeding – another variety containing the patented genetic material would come under control of the original patent.

In the US, many plant patents have already been granted. They can be taken out not only on newly developed varieties, but on heirlooms that have not previously been named and mar-keted, so that large seed companies are gaining the rights to seeds that have been in families for generations. In Europe at present, plant varieties are not patentable as such. However, the scope of PBR has been widened so that farmers and growers no longer have an automatic right freely to save seed of varieties covered by PBR, and its use by plant breeders is already restricted.

Neither PBR nor patents take account of the rights of local communities and indigenous peoples. It is their skill and knowledge that developed the landraces and traditional varieties which are the basis of modern breeding programmes. Varieties with desirable traits can be taken freely from countries in the centres of diversity by plant breeders in industrial countries, and used to create new varieties with the same traits. These effectively become the property of the large seed companies, and bring in revenue through patents or PBR. Often the varieties are sold back to the countries where the material originated, so, instead of being rewarded for their important contribution in developing them, the farmers may be required to pay to use the patented seed.

Farmers' rights, arising from their efforts in conserving and improving the genetic resources in their own countries, have been recognised internationally, but are still undervalued. Any system of reward has yet to be implemented, and the whole question is the subject of on-going international debate. Taking out patents on their own resources is beyond the means of farmers and community groups, and it is often also against their spiritual and ethical beliefs.

It is also outside the scope of specialist plant breeders such as the small companies developing varieties for biodynamic growing. Many large companies in the US are already spending considerable amounts of time and money in lawsuits defending their patents. Far from stimulating research, strict controls on access to genetic resources stifle innovation and threaten biodiversity. Our existing vegetable heritage has come about through the sharing of seeds and knowledge between individuals, communities and countries far more freely than patents would allow.

Illegal vegetables

Besides the legislation governing PBR, the countries in the European Union have additional laws controlling which vegetable varieties can and cannot be sold. No variety can legally be marketed unless it is registered on the National List of one of these countries. These regulations were designed to protect consumers from rogue seed traders, and to clear up genuine confusion, by ensuring that varieties were what they claimed to be. Thus carrot seeds from any packet labelled Autumn King must by law always produce plants of that variety. Similarly, companies cannot market Autumn King seed but call it Charlie's Carrot or some other name of their own. In theory, these guarantees are desirable for seed suppliers and growers, but in practice the effect of the legislation has been reduction in choice through the loss of many old varieties.

When the system was first set up in the early 1970s, seed companies were invited to submit names from their catalogues for listing, and some old varieties were automatically included without charge. Many, however, were not. These included family heirlooms, and other varieties not commercially available in Europe. Hundreds of those originally listed have also since been dropped.

In 1980 a Common European Catalogue was published, amalgamating National Lists from all EC countries. Over 1500 varieties, said to be identical to others but registered under different names, were struck from the list. It has since been estimated that only about one-third of these were genuine duplicates; others were distinctly or subtly different. Once a variety was dropped, it became illegal to supply it, no matter how valuable it might be (*see Up-to-Date Onion, right*).

DISHONEST SEED TRADING

In the last century sharp practices in the UK seed trade were not uncommon, as illustrated by a letter to a gardening journal in 1858:

'Last spring I purchased … a packet of [Cottager's Kale] seed so highly commended. It was sown and tended with due care, but it has turned out a parcel of the greatest rubbish that ever a man put in his garden. Had I been singular, I would have thought some accident had occurred whereby the seed had become mixed, but I know of several cases as bad as my own… There are no two plants from the seed alike: some are like the old Rag Jacks, others appear to be a bad cross between a purple cabbage and Curled Greens; but the whole are worthless.'

UP-TO-DATE ONION

Bred in England almost a century ago, this strongly flavoured onion is resistant to white rot – a disease affecting nearly all crops in the onion family. Up-to-Date was sold commercially in the UK until the 1970s, when it was dropped in favour of Bedfordshire Champion, to which it looked identical in trials. However, Bedfordshire Champion only appeared the same because there was no threat from white rot, to which it has little resistance.

Luckily Up-to-Date was kept in cultivation by a seed saving organisation.

AUBERGINES

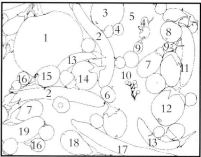

1. New York Spineless

2. Pingtung Long

3. Large White

4. Red Ruffled

5. Purple Pickling

6. Turkish Orange

7. Listada di Gandia

8. Laotian Green Stripe

9. Easter Egg

10. Laotian Grape

11. Long White

12. Rosa Bianca

13. Thai Green

14. Large White

15. White Oval

16. Ronde de Valence

17. Chinese Long Sword

18. Black Egg

19. Kurume Long Purple

Every variety on the market in Europe since the 1970s has had to be registered, requiring substantial fees, and strict testing. First it must pass a DUS test: it must be Distinct from all other varieties; it must be Uniform – all the plants of that particular variety must be the same, and it must be Stable – it must not change from generation to generation. Many old varieties, whilst being distinct strains, are not sufficiently uniform to satisfy the legislation.

The registration process itself is expensive, and there is an annual maintenance fee to keep the variety on the list. In the UK it costs around £1000 to register a new variety on the National List, and £300 a year to maintain it there. These fees are the same regardless how many packets of the seed are sold, whether it is a kale bought only by a few gardeners, or a cabbage grown by commercial growers over thousands of acres. Small independent seed companies who would like to start selling re-discovered heritage varieties, or new varieties bred just for home gardeners, find that these fees make it completely uneconomic.

The zeal with which the letter of the law is enforced varies from country to country. Thompson & Morgan, one of the biggest companies in the UK supplying seeds to home gardeners, has been prosecuted and fined by the UK Ministry of Agriculture, Fisheries and Food (MAFF) for selling varieties that were not on the National List. These were giant vegetables – a cucumber, cabbage, carrot and pumpkin – which particularly interested gardeners entering produce in local shows and other competitions. The varieties had failed the DUS test because they were not sufficiently uniform: some of the cucumbers had white prickles and some had black; some of the cabbages had more red veining than others; the carrots varied too much in size for the Ministry's liking, and the pumpkins varied too much in colour.

TM/M05 GREEN GRAPE TOMATO

Green Grape is a modern tomato variety, but it is often considered a heritage variety as it was selected in the US from a cross of an heirloom and a traditional variety (see Part Two, the Directory, page 159), and was released there in 1986. The vigorous plants produce small cherry fruits, renowned for their flavour. When ripe, they are green with yellow veining, resembling large Muscat grapes – hence their name.

In Europe Green Grape cannot legally be sold by name because it is not listed in the Common European Catalogue. Regardless of this, in 1997 it was introduced into the catalogue of the UK seed company Thompson & Morgan under the number TM/M05, and gardeners who buy seed receive a form to fill in about the variety's performance. This makes selling the seed legal because the tomato is 'under trial'.

MAFF also interprets the word 'market' in the legislation very strictly. At least one British company has been prevented from giving away unlisted seeds, inferring that this change of ownership of the seeds constitutes marketing. The main UK seed saving group, the HDRA, calls its seed collection a 'Library', with gardeners paying a membership fee but getting 'free' seeds; so far the Ministry has chosen not to prosecute. Other European countries appear to be more relaxed about the seed regulations, or to interpret them in different ways – varieties that are not on the EC list certainly feature in some Italian and French seed catalogues directed at gardeners rather than commercial growers. But in general, the existence of the law is enough to prevent small companies from maintaining and selling unlisted heritage varieties.

Nevertheless, there are ways of bending the rules. Reasonable quantities of seeds may be distributed for trial purposes, so seed companies can put an unlisted variety in their catalogue under a trial number, and ask customers to report back on its performance (*see opposite page*). Distributing seeds may be illegal, but distributing plants is not, and selling young plants of unlisted varieties through the post is becoming fairly commonplace. Even chitted seeds (seeds which have just germinated and have a small white rootlet showing) can be marketed.

Changes to the European law have been suggested – such as the creation of an official Heirloom List, or a list of varieties marketable in small quantities for gardeners, and there are signs that this may happen, but EC bureaucracy works painfully slowly. Meanwhile, each year more and more familiar open-pollinated varieties become outlaws: Cottager's Kale (deleted in 1992), Canadian Wonder French bean (in 1993), Sunset runner bean (in 1994), Hero of Lockinge melon (in 1995), Snow White cauliflower (in 1996)... and many more.

SAVING THE CZAR

When varieties have been cultivated by gardeners for decades it is usually for good reason, and the latest commercial varieties offered by the seed companies cannot always replace them.

This was certainly true of the Czar, a white-flowered runner bean with long, almost stringless pods, introduced in the UK at the end of the 19th century. It had enduring popularity with gardeners, possibly because it had white seeds which were very good for drying as well as tender fleshy pods. It featured in seed catalogues for nearly 100 years before, in 1988, it was threatened with deletion from the National List. It took a determined campaign by the Henry Doubleday Research Association to persuade one seed company to save it.

As a consequence the Czar is now legitimately undergoing a revival as a heritage variety, but others have not been so lucky. The melon Hero of Lockinge was introduced by the seed firm Carters in 1881 as the 'finest new melon of the season'. It has beautiful yellow fruit, with flesh that is almost white and very tender – one of the varieties grown in the melon houses of Victorian kitchen gardens, remaining a favourite for over a century. But in 1995 it was dropped from the National List. Now it is illegal for anyone to sell the seed.

ORIENTAL
GREENS

Oriental Brassicas, Pak
Choi and hardy Mustards
are among the fast-growing
Oriental vegetables which
provide a wide choice of
fresh salad and stir-fry
greens when other leafy
vegetables are limited.

Industrial food production

The combination of modern farming methods and the nationwide marketing of fresh produce has meant an inevitable concentration on fewer vegetable varieties. Whereas previously farmers would have produced a wide mix of crops over a long harvest period, increased mechanisation and the use of chemicals make it much easier, and more profitable, for them to grow large areas of just a few varieties.

In most industrialised nations only a small proportion of fresh produce is marketed locally through small greengrocers or farm shops. Many farmers now grow to the demands of the supermarket chains, which have taken over an increasing share of this market from greengrocers – over 50% in the UK in 1996, for example, compared to only 24% in 1993. The major food stores want to buy in bulk – large quantities of a uniform crop at a specified date – and are not interested in any variety that is only grown in small amounts, or that does not travel well, or have a long shelf life. In order to satisfy these demands, farmers are increasingly under pressure to grow a narrow band of crops which ripen uniformly, all look the same, and are easy to harvest by machine.

As more food is sold in a ready-to-eat form, the demands of the food processors also have an influence. Whereas at home we happily adjust recipes, oven temperatures and cooking times to suit a great variation in produce, processors match their machinery and production lines to a few suitable varieties, further limiting the number which they find acceptable. So the food processors, not the growers or consumers, are important in determining which potatoes are planted, for example, as only a few varieties are suitable for them to make crisps or oven chips.

As consumers, it is all too easy to get caught up in the system – to buy washed and prepacked vegetables because they are eye-catchingly displayed, and to use pre-prepared and precooked dishes because they are quick and simple.

Cooking a meal used to mean taking fresh raw ingredients and turning them into a dish, but this happens less and less. To many people, the communal meal and the traditions and values associated with food appear, sadly, to be less and less important. Some have never been taught to cook the commonest vegetables, let alone sweet potatoes or salsify. The food processors and supermarkets decide what they eat, and hence what the farmers grow, and how.

In developing countries, modern farming methods and associated development such as roadbuilding and dams, have had drastic consequences for genetic diversity and local communities. As fields are enlarged and chemicals are used, not only are traditional varieties displaced but native wild plants in the field margins are destroyed. These include many which are important to the local diet and culture. Peasant farmers, who cared for the old varieties for centuries, are turned off their lands so that the landlords can increase their acreages. High value 'cash crops' for export are often grown in preference to local vegetable crops.

The effects can be startling: for example, the area round the Aral Sea is part of the Central Asian centre of diversity – the home of many melons, onions, garlic, carrots, radishes, turnips and other crops. The Aral Sea was once the fourth largest inland sea in the world, but during the 1930s all the rivers flowing into it were diverted to irrigate monocultures of cotton. Now the sea has lost 60% of its surface. The soil on the exposed sea bed contains high levels of pesticides and salts which are blown around in desert dust storms, contaminating plant and animal life for hundreds and possibly thousands of miles around.

CHILLI BEANS
AND MAIZE TACOS

*Following the 1995 Rio
conference on Biodiversity, one
UK environmental group,
SAFE Alliance, published a
paper illustrating how
traditional agriculture
maintains diversity, whilst
modern food production
systems work against it. This
is one of their examples.*

*Chilli beans and maize tacos
form a meal that can be
bought, ready-made, in many
US and European supermar-
kets. It is also a typical main
meal of Mexican peasants.
However, everything about the
way the two meals are
produced is different.*

*The Mexican peasant grows
the maize and the beans
together and the tomatoes and
chillies at the side, in a mixed
cropping pattern that makes the
best use of the soil nutrients
and minimises the spread of
pests and diseases. Several
varieties of each species are used
– each with differing resistance
to variations in climate and to
pests and disease, so whatever
the conditions, some of the crop
will provide a good yield.*

*Industrial agriculture grows
separate large areas of maize,
beans, tomatoes and chillies,
each area containing a single
variety; chemical fertilisers are
applied to supply nutrients and
pests and diseases are controlled
by spraying. The food man-
ufacturer buys in the four
genetically uniform ingredients
in the world market so that
each of the ingredients might
conceivably even come from a
different continent.*

Modern marketing

Farmers in developing countries can usually be persuaded that the latest seeds which come with outstanding promises are superior to their traditional local varieties, which quickly become something to be ashamed of. Representatives from some major companies are eager to capitalise on this attitude.

Seed Savers International (SSI) is a project linking Seed Savers Exchange, Arche Noah, (the genetic preservation organisation in Austria), and seed banks in Eastern Europe. Recently, when one of their members was searching for endangered varieties in a remote mountainous area of northern Poland, he discovered that representatives from commercial Dutch seed companies had recently preceded him even there. They had been attempting to sell peasant farmers the latest hybrid varieties, encouraging them to change from their traditional tried-and-tested crops.

In Europe and the US, many gardeners are similarly lured by glossy catalogues and glowing descriptions. In mainstream gardening circles, growing the old favourites can often be seen as unfashionable, and saving seeds to provide for next year's sowings may be considered at the least eccentric, and at the worst as an indication of poverty. Yet for our ancestors it was an integral part of the cycle of growing their own food, and of developing new varieties.

It is not necessary to turn the clock back, so that everyone must save all their own seeds. But neither can the process be left to a few multinational companies. More people – small seed companies, individual farmers, growers and gardeners – with varying interests and different ways of growing plants, need to be involved in seed production and plant breeding. Only then will diversity be maintained and our food supply become less vulnerable.

POSITIVE GROWTH

ABOVE: *The diversity of sweet potatoes is so great that some will even thrive in temperate climates.*

LEFT: *Tender shoots of asparagus emerge in spring to provide a welcome treat full of the promise of summer.*

The main official response to the threat of lost genes has been to collect endangered varieties and put them into long-term storage in gene banks. One of the first and most important collections of such genetic material was assembled by the Russian botanist Vavilov and his colleagues. Their travels to collect plants during the 1920s and 30s in particular led Vavilov to identify the centres of diversity of our crops (*see page 21*), and made him realise the crucial importance of preserving them. The Vavilov Institute of Plant Industry in St Petersburg has more than 360,000 seed samples from countries around the world.

In 1943 Vavilov died in a Soviet prison, a martyr to his scientific beliefs, and many of his colleagues also perished under Stalin's regime. Stories of heroism abound: apparently up to 14 scientists died at their desks at the Institute during the German siege of Leningrad, starving to death rather than eating any of the seeds around them, which they saw as indispensable resources for the future. Their work was, and is, an inspiration to other scientists.

Many countries worldwide have now set up gene banks, some housing predominantly local varieties, others carrying a range of crops from a wide area. The Nordic gene bank in Sweden, for example, concentrates on varieties from the Scandinavian region, whereas the UK gene bank maintains world collections of radish, onions, carrots and many cultivated brassicas. In the US, the National Seed Storage Laboratory (NSSL) houses nearly 400,000 seed samples from recent and traditional varieties, and from wild species of all main crops grown in North America.

Gene banks store seeds under cold dry conditions. Seed is typically dried to 5% moisture content, hermetically sealed in foil packets, and stored at -20°C (-4°F). Under these conditions, the seeds of some vegetables will remain viable even after 25 years, although their potential to germinate will gradually decrease. In the NSSL, some seeds destined for long-term storage are packed into small tubes and their temperature lowered to -160°C (-256°F) using liquid nitrogen.

Periodically the seeds must be grown out: a proportion of the seed of each variety is sown and grown, then new seed is collected and returned to the bank. Some crops can be grown out in nearby open plots, but others must be kept in glasshouses, or isolated in tunnels covered with insect-proof netting to prevent cross-pollination. Potato varieties must be grown from seed potatoes rather than botanical seed to keep them true to type, so they have to be stored as tubers in a cold-room and regenerated annually, or kept under laboratory conditions in tissue culture.

This hi-tech solution to saving our vegetable heritage is one important approach, but it has some major drawbacks. Collections in gene banks can inevitably only represent a sample of what actually exists in cultivation and in the wild. Sometimes the selection is deliberate, focusing on immediate rather than longterm solutions – varieties are specifically sought for characteristics that are commercially important at the time, such as a specific disease resistance. Other seed collecting missions, although more eclectic, are very often limited by time or money, or by the social or physical conditions in the areas where they take place.

Gene banks can only be as safe as the technology upon which they rely – some are in areas with unpredictable electricity supplies, for example – and they are vulnerable to deliberate sabotage and accidental damage. In recognition of this, collections are usually, but not always, duplicated in more than one gene bank in more than one country. The Nordic gene bank have also set up a secure long-term store which does not rely on a power supply – in a steel container deep within an abandoned mine gallery in Svålbard within the Arctic Circle. The gallery has a 70m (230 ft) thick roof and a naturally sta-ble temperature, generally between -1°C (30°F) and -4°C (25°F).

However, by far the greatest danger to gene banks is lack of government funding, and lack of clear policies for the future. In Canada, 1995 budget cuts closed or curtailed the activities of some of the country's gene banks. In under-developed countries the funding is usually precarious. Many European gene banks suffer from lack of resources, and even the NSSL, the US's most important collection of genetic material, is dangerously underfunded. This means that seed samples are not being grown out or evaluated as often as they should be. Seeds are actually dying in storage. There is a need for clear international agreement on a coherent policy, and consistent funding.

Another problem in gene banks is ensuring that the genetic diversity in the stored seeds is preserved. The number of seeds grown out to renew a sample that is deteriorating will only be a small percentage of those originally collected, and is unlikely to represent the full genetic picture. For example, an initial sample of the seed of wild potato species stored at the Scottish Crops Research Institute might contain enough seed to generate about 20,000 plants, but only about 40 are used to regenerate the sample.

Some seeds will also store better than others, and some plants will do better than others when grown out – in conditions which may be quite different to those in the region where the seed sample was collected. Thus as time goes on, varieties adapt to conditions in the gene bank, rather than evolving to meet changes in the environment, or in pest and disease organisms in the outside world.

Gene banks are one vital resource in conserving biodiversity, but they are the preserve of scientists and at the mercy of government policies. Conservation is also vital at the grassroots level, on farms and in gardens, and there is now increasing awareness of this. International organisations, individual countries and states, and, in particular, pressure groups and local communities, are all responding. On many fronts positive action is being taken. It is beginning to make a difference.

Field and garden conservation

When an unexpected outbreak of wart disease struck UK potato crops in 1910, inspectors noticed that amongst the many varieties in cultivation the variety Golden Wonder was immune. From this variety other resistant varieties were bred. If only a few varieties had been growing, and the rest had been kept in gene banks, the chances are that a variety with this valuable trait would never have been discovered. It is essential to maintain vegetable diversity where it belongs – in gardens and on farms. Then crops will naturally adapt and evolve, and we can assess how they perform under a wide range of conditions.

This value of diversity, and the importance of local farming and gardening methods in preserving it, is at last beginning to be recognised, particularly in the developing world, where local attitudes are moving away from the ideas of the Green Revolution (*see page 48*). In such countries there is often a great diversity in traditional crops, and the problem is to dispel the myth that what comes from outside is better.

One of many successful initiatives has taken place in the Chiloe Islands, off Southern Chile. These are considered as one of the centres of origin of the potato, but over the last few decades local varieties have gradually been displaced by modern ones. In an attempt to halt this loss of the traditional crops, in 1989, a community-supported 'living gene bank' of native varieties was planted. Within a few years seed potatoes from this programme were being distributed to farmers, who quickly discovered the advantages of the old varieties: they do well under a wide range of conditions, taste better, and use less fuel to cook. Now, rather than relying on external initiatives, the farmers are selling and exchanging seed amongst themselves.

NATIVE SEEDS/SEARCH

Native Seeds/SEARCH (NSS) is a non-profit organisation working to collect rare, wild, and heritage Native American plant species and varieties. The stated mission of the NSS is to 'conserve and promote the use of native or adapted agriculturally valuable plants, and to establish by research their cultural, nutritive and ecological value'.

NSS store and distribute the seeds of these native plants, both locally and globally. While the seeds are available to any interested growers, Native American groups receive seeds free of charge; this is the NSS way of thanking the thousands of original seed savers, the native tribes who nurtured indigenous species, and preserved them, keeping their culinary traditions and folklore intact.

In addition to gifts of seeds, NSS organises and participates in education and cultivation programmes, and actively encourages the native peoples of the South West to grow their traditional native seeds. These are adapted to the desert, the mountains and poor soils. Many native species naturally tolerate droughts and pests and diseases, and in the less-than-ideal conditions of the arid Southwest, native seeds will always outperform modern non-adapted varieties.

WINTER SQUASH

1. Longfellow

2. Futtsu

3. White Cushaw

4. Early Large Yellow Paris

5. Rouge Vif D'Etampes

6. Ucon Acorn

7. Striped Cordebese

8. Candystick

9. Gold Striped Cushaw

10. White Acorn

11. Whangaparoa Crown

12. American Indian

13. Tatume

14. Tarahumara Indian

15. Mandan

16. Campêche

17. Fordhook

18. Triamble

Seed savers' networks

It is often personal experience that prompts people to action, to keep alive the link between plants and people, and resist the loss of our vegetable heritage.

In 1971 Diane Whealy's grandfather gave her and her husband Kent the seed of three plants that his family had brought with them to the US from Bavaria four generations before. These were two vegetables – a large German tomato and a prolific climbing bean – and a beautiful dark strain of the flower Morning Glory. The old man, Grandpa Ott, died that winter, and Kent and Diane realised that it was up to them to keep the heirlooms alive. Kent then began to write to gardening magazines in an attempt to locate other people who might be keeping seeds passed on to them by their families, and from this small start grew the Seed Savers Exchange (SSE), the largest seed savers' network in the world, dedicated to saving endangered vegetable varieties. Their companion Flower and Herb Exchange fulfils the same role for flowers and herbs.

In the UK, it was the insidious progress of plant breeders' rights and the seed regulations that rang alarm bells to one man – Lawrence Hills. Lawrence was founder of the Henry Doubleday Research Association (HDRA) established to research and promote organic growing, and under their auspices he campaigned for the country's vanishing vegetables and launched a Seed Library to make heritage varieties available to gardeners and growers throughout the country. To the 7,800 members of HDRA's Heritage Seed Programme, Lawrence Hills cries to 'Save the Czar', a traditional white-flowered runner bean (*see page 69*), and other vegetables which were in danger of being dropped from the National List, are now legendary.

Michel and Jude Fanton started Seed Savers' Network in Australia when they began to search for particular varieties and found they were not available through any recognised seed supplier in Australia. Advertisements in gardening magazines provoked such a great response that the Fantons were inundated with offers of seeds and information. So they decided to share this wealth with other gardeners, while continuing to build up reserves of heritage varieties from every possible source.

In Austria, Nancy Arrowsmith runs the seed savers' network Arche Noah (Noah's Ark), now the only privately owned seed supplier in Austria. And in the Netherlands the Court of Eden encourages people to grow as many varieties as possible from their extraordinarily diverse collection of seeds.

As well as acting as seed suppliers and seed banks, Arche Noah and Seed Savers International – part of SSE – have jointly arranged several expeditions to collect endangered vegetables in Eastern Europe and the Mediterranean. Over the last few years losses of traditional varieties have been occurring in these centres of diversity at an alarming rate, and the national gene banks in most of the countries concerned are not in a position to do any collecting themselves, with few facilities and limited funding for the maintenance of varieties.

These and the other seed savers' networks that grew up in the 1970s and 80s have various features in common which distinguish them from official gene banks. They do not collect seeds according to currently relevant criteria, such as the specific needs of industrial agricultural systems, but collect and receive as wide a range of varieties as possible. Rather than collecting in order to store seeds away for some future date, networks want to make the seed available to everyone – they want the seeds to be used. Through growing the seeds, using the vegetables, saving some seed each year and redistributing it, gardeners will bring the old varieties back into common use.

The members of seed savers' networks in Europe and North America between them maintain and exchange thousands of varieties of traditional vegetable varieties. For example, the 1997 yearbook of Seed Savers Exchange lists about 12,000 varieties and the addresses of 1,000 members who are offering these to other gardeners. Some of these varieties are family heirlooms, others have particular historic value; few are available from commercial catalogues.

Sometimes remarkable heritage varieties have simply turned up in the post. When Jeremy Cherfas was running HDRA's Heritage Seed Programme, he described how one morning he received a bulky padded envelope containing not seeds, but two turnips about to run to flower. A note inside from the sender of the rather smelly package said that the turnips were an old commercial variety called Laird's Victory, kept going for decades by his neighbour who had recently died at the age of 90. The seeds had been thrown out by relatives clearing up – all that remained was the turnips in the garden.

Often, however, it has taken a more determined search to find old varieties. The investigations of the Swedish seed saving group SESAM led to the discovery of six local landraces of broad beans (field or *fava* beans), although the Nordic gene bank had only one. Peter Erlandsson of SESAM also describes how he also rescued a local grey pea variety from a province in the south of the Netherlands. The 11 seeds which he obtained were about 40 years old – but 10 of them germinated, so the stock could be renewed. Other Swedish heirlooms have been repatriated to SESAM from Seed Savers' Exchange in the US (*see above, right*).

ESTHER'S SWEDISH BEAN

This drying bean is a heritage variety from a family that emigrated from Sweden and settled in Montana, US. It is a vigorous hardy plant, which thrives in cold climates, and produces a good crop of brown-yellow beans. The variety was kept in cultivation through Seed Savers Exchange in the US, and eventually repatriated to the Swedish seed savers' network SESAM.

BATH SEED SAVERS

The virtual disappearance of the Bath Cos lettuce led gardeners in Bath, in Southwest England, to form a local seed saving group. Small local groups are often best placed to save varieties with such specific associations.

BRASSICAS

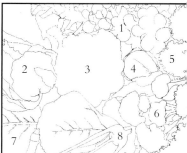

1. Long Island Improved
   Brussels Sprouts

2. Andes Cauliflower

3. Sicilian Purple Cauliflower

4. Evergreen Ballhead Cabbage

5. Siberian Kale

6. De Cicco Broccoli

7. Georgia Collards

8. Early Purple Vienna
   Kohl Rabi

Alternative markets

Even if you can't grow your food yourself, you can increase the choice of what you eat by buying direct from farmers and market gardeners. Marketing vegetables directly to consumers allows growers to produce small quantities of a greater range of crops and varieties, and vegetables do not have to travel, or look perfect.

There are now over 2,400 local farmers' markets in the US, and it is estimated that over 4 million consumers get a portion of their fresh produce from them. They offer the chance to buy fresh locally grown food, and to try out produce not found in shops. Much of Europe has a long and thriving tradition of local vegetable markets, and you can also buy direct from the producers in other ways.

In the UK, there has been a huge rise in 'vegetable box schemes' during the past few years. Under these schemes, fixed price boxes of organically grown seasonal produce are delivered directly to customers. Generally one grower, or a group of several local growers, will produce nearly all the produce to fill the boxes, and a close relationship builds up with the consumers. This offers the chance of growing what people want, and the opportunity for growers and customers to try something different.

Another exciting way forward is the rise of community supported farms, a more radical way to become involved with those who are growing the produce. Community members contribute financially directly to the farm by buying a share in the produce before it is grown, and participating in decisions about what is grown. In the US in particular, the number of such projects is growing steadily. They nearly always result in an increase in the range of what is grown, and make the members more aware of the intrinsic value of diversity.

CHEFS AND RESTAURANTS

All over Europe and North America, chefs are increasingly using traditional vegetables – in California there are several restaurants using little but heirloom varieties. In France, at least one prestigious hotel chain with restaurants in and around Paris, has started including old varieties in its menu. This has helped to save varieties such as the Green Paris artichoke (Gros Vert de Laon), popular in the last century but shunned in recent years because it is less productive for market gardening than modern counterparts. The century-old cabbage Chou de Saint-Saens, has also been recently rediscovered and taken up by local restaurants.

Sooke Harbour House, a fine restaurant on Vancouver Island in British Columbia, uses only seasonal produce grown within a 30 mile radius. Their dishes include many local plants eaten by Native Americans, such as the flat-leaved nodding onion (Allium cernum), and Indian celery (Lomantium nudicale), as well as other traditional crops. One favourite is the Gourgane bean, a local broad bean with very thin-skinned beans.

In the UK, several chefs are now emphasising organically produced traditional varieties of vegetables; the principles is that if you use old varieties you are already halfway to creating a tasty meal, and it is therefore easier to succeed.

Small seed companies

Although the pressures described in earlier chapters have dangerously depleted resources, the regeneration of interest in our heritage is beginning to encourage the growth of a number of small seed companies selling open-pollinated and endangered varieties. The situation in North America is particularly optimistic. Here, with a bit of sleuthing, you can find fascinating heirlooms of most vegetables. Some suppliers dedicate themselves to saving and marketing varieties of one species – several specialise in tomatoes and peppers, or beans, corns, or squashes. One individual, Ted Mackza (the Fish Lake Garlic Man), is dedicated to making Canada 'self-sufficient in garlic'; other growers are equally proud of their own specialities.

At the time of writing, legislation in Europe makes the marketing of old varieties more difficult (*see Chapter Three*). Nevertheless, an increasing number of small companies are seeking out and selling legal traditional varieties, or finding ways around the laws. There are also optimistic signs that legislation may soon be changed to allow more varieties to be sold.

A number of small seed companies in mainland Europe and the US are now specialising in selling 'biodynamically' produced seed. Biodynamics is a system of growing put forward by the German philosopher Rudolf Steiner – a type of organic growing which recognises the energy cycles of plants and the role of cosmic forces. There are no hybrids in the biodynamic catalogues, and many contain old regional varieties which were developed before the advent of chemicals in agriculture.

If you support small specialist seed suppliers, and buy varieties that are endangered by modern hybrids, these varieties are much less likely to disappear.

THOMAS ETTY ESQ

This small UK seed company has a catalogue of nearly 150 heritage varieties, most of them introduced into Europe between 1800 and 1900, although the oldest, Painted Lady runner bean, is said to date from 1633. The company was began by Ray Warner who painstakingly researched the history of the varieties and sourced supplies, and gave it the name of his great great great great grandfather, Thomas Etty. He had been a 'general dealer' in the North of England, and probably sold some of the same vegetables.

VITALIS

A forward-thinking small seed company recently established in the Netherlands, Vitalis grows biodynamically and trials open-pollinated varieties from many sources worldwide, sometimes from gene banks. Those which are particularly suitable for organic and biodynamic growing are selected – such as those with good disease resistance, and which respond well to organic manuring. Vitalis also carry out some cross-pollination in order to develop new varieties, helping to maintain diversity in varieties brought to the market.

SEEDS

A handful of bean seeds is a geat illustration of vegetable diversity. All colours and sizes are here, with varieties suitable for cool climates, hot areas, fresh eating, shelling, slicing, or drying.

Bean seeds are easy to save and store, and many varieties will still germinate after several years' storage.

Living museums

Many of the seed-saving organisations have gardens where you can see heritage vegetables growing. SSE has a 170 acre farm in Iowa, which includes an orchard and wildlife park, as well as a garden containing around 1,500 vegetable varieties grown annually for seed in the $2^{1/2}$ acres of grounds by the centre.

In the UK a network of period gardens grows varieties maintained by HDRA's Heritage Seed Programme. For example, the gardens of the impressive 16th century Sudeley Castle in Gloucestershire, England, are growing varieties that were popular prior to the last century. The Apprentice House Garden, part of a working museum of the cotton industry at Quarry Bank Mill, Styal in Cheshire, dates back to the 1790s and has vegetables appropriate to the time. The varieties grown have to adapt to modern conditions and usually to modern methods of cultivation; it is this interaction of the old and the new that helps to maintain and develop diversity.

In the US, a number of period gardens and farms play an important role in making people aware of their vegetable heritage. One of the best documented is that of the US's most famous farmer, Thomas Jefferson, at Monticello in Virginia. His vegetable garden was a 300 yard long, southeast facing terrace, where he experimented with hundreds of different varieties from many different countries. At one time he cultivated 15 varieties of English pea, for example. Jefferson recorded his gardening activities in the first part of the 19th century in great detail in a diary detailing his daily sowing and harvesting, and a 'garden book' with cultural notes, and many letters that he wrote. The garden has now been restored and opened to the public, after extensive research locating the types and varieties of vegetables he grew. Many of these can be seen growing, and seeds can be bought.

WEST DEAN GARDENS

West Dean is a grand old English country house surrounded by over 300 acres of parkland and ornamental gardens beneath the Sussex downs in Southern England. It has a $2^{1/2}$ acre walled kitchen garden, which in its heyday would have grown a wide range of produce for the household – family, servants and guests (Edward VII was a frequent visitor).

Good records exist, and in the early 1990s the walled kitchen garden and its 13 Victorian glasshouses were restored and planted, with the aim of recreating the original productive Edwardian kitchen garden. Many of the vegetables grown are contemporary – such as Green Windsor runner beans, and Flourball and Lord Rosebery potatoes.

However, the overall aim has been to display the possibilities of kitchen gardening and the range of plants available, rather than strict historical accuracy. As well as Edwardian plants, in the last few years visitors have been able to see nearly 100 different varieties of peppers and chillies and over 50 different tomatoes, as well as a wide range of other vegetables, mainly grown from seed supplied by the HDRA and SSE.

Community events

There is no better way to become aware of our endangered vegetable heritage than to see and taste the varieties. With this in mind, numerous events are organised by local communities and seedsaving groups, and even if you have no garden at all you can become involved.

Every October, Seed Savers Exchange hosts a Pumpkin Celebration at its Iowa farm, where pumpkins in many different shapes and sizes are available for carving. There is a huge bonfire, a dinner, and a procession with lighted pumpkins. Among other vegetable-oriented festivals, Native Seeds/SEARCH holds a pepper fiesta, and there are well attended garlic festivals in Europe and California. Your area might have other celebrations.

In the UK, the HDRA hold a Potato Day where over 100 varieties of seed potato are on sale. They include many varieties such as Edzell Blue and British Queen which are rarely seen in shops and garden centres today. Tubers are priced individually instead of being packed into kilo bags, so even if you only have a small garden, you have the opportunity to try lots of different varieties. Potato Day also includes talks, cookery demonstrations and displays of the old varieties from HDRA's Heritage Seed Programme.

At a local level, a simple way to introduce heritage varieties is to enter them in horticultural shows or bring them to similar community gatherings – pot luck suppers, bring and buys, harvest festivals. They may not win any prizes, but will certainly attract plenty of attention.

Events which focus on regional history and culture can also be a focus for traditional crops. For example, twice a year the Ecomusée in the town of La Corneuve in France holds its Marché au Musée, selling over 70 varieties of fruit and vegetables, all currently grown in the region. La Corneuve was once part of the largest vegetable producing plain of France (la Plaine des Vertus) where many regional varieties arose. These figure prominently in the market alongside modern introductions, and many dishes based on recipes from old cookery books are prepared for people to taste. The Marché au Musée encourages people to try traditional varieties, and hence helps persuade commercial producers to keep them in cultivation.

GARLIC FESTIVALS IN FRANCE

The French have been growing garlic for centuries, and there are many customs associated with it, particularly in the south-east of the country. Here it is traditionally planted on 10th November, and harvested on 20th June, and festivals associated with garlic occur at different venues in Provence throughout the summer.

The Foire de Saint Jean in Marseilles is the first of many, at the end of June, and many locals buy their garlic supply for the year during the fair, but possibly the most celebrated garlic festival takes place at the end of August at the town of Piolonc in central Provence. The surrounding area is reputed to grow the best garlic of all, on fertile plains below the rocky slopes, in fields intersown with strips of lavender.

Producers gather from all over Provence, tractors pull decorated trailers full of garlic around town, pavements are edged with strings of garlic bulbs, the whole town smells of garlic and local herbs as regional specialities are prepared in cafés and on pavements, and chefs race each other along the main street. All the local varieties are on sale – and for sampling – at stands throughout the town, but the old favourites are the traditional pink-striped Rose de Lautrec, and the very large bulbed white Blanc de Lomagne.

⑤

SAVING THE SEED

F ew gardeners now save seed of their own crops, yet this is the link which enables traditional varieties to be widely grown and heirlooms to be passed from generation to generation. Seed saving does not have to be complicated, and for many crops it is very easy, particularly those where the fruit or seed pods are also the edible part of the plant, such as tomatoes and beans. There is little difference between growing these crops for seed and growing them to eat – the main difficulty is usually stopping the family from picking them all!

Some climates pose limitations on growing certain crops for seed, particularly short-season areas, or where harvesting weather is unreliable, but, with a few years' experience, you can grow seed from most vegetables in most areas.

Saving the seed of some crops departs slightly from normal vegetable growing routine. You may need to grow crops in different places in the garden, for example, to isolate them from one another. You may need to leave them in the ground for much longer than you would to get an edible crop, and they may take up more space – a lettuce grown to eat is small and compact, but when left to seed it will send up flower stalks about a metre (3ft) tall. Your seed

ABOVE: *Purple-podded climbing beans came from France in the 18th century. They are hardy, productive and adaptable.*

LEFT: *Alliums growing for seed in one of the Preservation Gardens at Seed Savers Exchange, near Decorah, Iowa, USA.*

production will depend on the size of your garden, on the climate, and on how much time you have.

It is usually possible to save seed from the majority of common vegetables without much difficulty, although brassicas and sweetcorn pose particular problems. This short chapter aims to show you what is involved in seed saving, and to get you started with one or two easy crops. For detailed crop by crop information, you will need a more specialised book, and some are recommended in *Further Reading (pages 183-186)*.

Begin your seed growing with your favourite varieties, those which have proved to be well adapted to your environment, and to your personal taste. Be warned, seed saving is addictive – once you start, you will almost certainly want to carry on to do more. It is fascinating to watch plants that you do not normally see flowering run up to seed. Some of the seed heads – the white umbels of the carrot, for example, and the architectural spheres of the leek – are also surprisingly attractive, and are loved by bees and other beneficial insects. Above all, it is extremely rewarding to have seed from your own crops to sow next year, and extra to give away to friends and neighbours.

Annual, biennial or perennial

One of the important characteristics you need to know about a vegetable before you consider saving it for seed, is whether it is annual, biennial or perennial.

Annual crops are those that are started from seed each year and produce flowers and seeds within one season of growth. They are usually sown in spring and give seeds in autumn – which fits in well with the growing cycle in the vegetable garden. Lettuce, peas and spinach are just a few of the many crops that come into this category. Where the growing season is short, some annual crops may need to be grown in a greenhouse or tunnel in order to produce seed.

Biennial crops do not go to seed until their second growing season, after a period of winter cold. For seed crops it is best to sow them in late summer so they bolt in the spring. Biennials include most winter brassicas, spinach beet, leeks, onions, and roots such as carrots and parsnips. Roots and onions often need to be lifted and stored over winter, and replanted the following spring. Leafy crops are best left in place in the garden, although this is a problem in cold climates where winter temperatures can be too low for them to survive.

Perennial crops do not have to be propagated from seed each year, and are thus not difficult to maintain. They include those that grow on in the same place year after year such as globe artichokes, asparagus, sea kale and tree onions, and those which we dig up from the vegetable plot each year, but which are propagated from tubers or offsets – potatoes, Jerusalem artichokes, garlic and shallots, for example. These last crops are particularly easy to multiply and pass on, but they run the risk of accumulating virus diseases. Some plants, such as tomatoes, that are actually perennials are treated as annuals in cold climates.

Keeping the variety pure

In order to produce seed, a flower must be pollinated: the stigma of the flower (the female part) must receive pollen from the anthers (the male part) either of the same or a different flower. Some crops self-pollinate – pollen is transferred within the same flower resulting in fertilisation. Others cross-pollinate – pollen is brought from another flower, usually by the wind or by insects. If the pollen comes from a different variety of the same crop species, then plants from the resulting seed will be a cross between the two varieties and not true to type.

In peas and beans self-pollination occurs before the flowers even open, making saving pure seed particularly easy. Peppers will also self-pollinate, but in addition cross-pollination by insects often occurs. If you are growing more than one variety of pepper, you must therefore take steps to isolate the varieties in some way to ensure pure seed. Brassicas are the most outgoing; most have a mechanism that prevents self-pollination, and for a flower to set seed it must have pollen brought by insects not just from a different flower, but from a flower on a different plant. One brassica plant on its own, even if it has many flowers, will produce little if any seed.

Separation distances

If you want to save seed from two varieties of the same species flowering at the same time, they must be separated by a distance large enough to prevent contamination by insects or wind-blown pollen. It is not only pollen from your own crops that you have to consider, but that from your neighbours' crops, and possibly from weeds of the same botanical family. Carrots will cross with wild carrots, for example, and cabbages, cauliflowers, broccoli, kale, Brussels sprouts and kohl rabi will all cross-pollinate with one another and with some field brassicas and their escapees in the wild.

Necessary isolation distances vary widely from crop to crop. French beans, which self-pollinate and rarely cross, only need a minimal distance of a few metres between two varieties to keep the seed pure. Cabbages, on the other hand, usually need to be separated from similar flowering brassicas by around 500m (550yds); commercially minimum distances of around a kilometre (1100yds) are required. These distances will also depend on other factors such as how many insects there are around, and what else there is for them to feed on. Obstacles between crops such as hedges, buildings and other barriers can also reduce the chances of cross-pollination, but this is not guaranteed.

Physical barriers

An alternative to isolating crops by distance is to use physical barriers. If you require only small amounts of seed it is simplest to cover individual flowers or flower clusters with a bag – this works well for peppers, for example. Use paper bags or pieces of horticultural fleece, never polythene bags, as these create a hot humid atmosphere and encourage the flowers to rot. Alternatively, whole plants or even groups of plants can be caged to keep out pollinating insects. You can make cheap cages from wood covered with shade netting or fine nylon mesh.

Remember that since both bags and cages keep out insects, flowers inside them that are not self-pollinating will normally need pollinating by hand. Or you can stop two varieties that are growing alongside one another from cross-pollinating, and yet still allow insects to work them, by caging them on alternate days. Whilst the first is caged, insects can pollinate the second and vice versa. Swap the cages at night.

Selecting plants

Always save seed from as many plants of a variety as possible, even if just one would give enough seed for your needs. Otherwise there is a risk of decreasing the genetic diversity within the crop. Some vegetables are more sensitive to this danger than others. Those that usually self-pollinate, such as tomatoes, lettuce, peas and beans have little natural variation within any one variety. You could successfully save seed from just a couple of plants – although it is preferable to use about six. At the other end of the scale, crops such as sweetcorn and onions deteriorate markedly if seed is saved from too few plants. At least 20 onions and 100 corn plants of any one variety are needed for seed saving, otherwise its variability will be lost and undesirable traits may appear.

You also need extra plants to allow you to select the best, and to 'rogue' out any which are not true to type or have unwanted character-istics. You should always choose vigorous healthy plants for seed saving, but other criteria for selecting 'the best' are not always as straight-forward. You need to look at the whole plant, not just the part you eat, and consider such characteristics as pest and disease resistance, drought resistance, resistance to bolting, and harvest time. For example, the first lettuces that produce flower spikes are not the ones to select, however tempting that may be, because the seed saved from these plants will probably give lettuces that also bolt early giving only a short harvest period.

If you are maintaining a heritage variety, you will want to choose the strongest and most typical plants to use for saving seed, then the most desirable characteristics will be passed to future generations.

Seed collecting and cleaning

Fruiting crops that have seeds embedded in moist flesh must be harvested when the fruits are fully mature. For pumpkins, this is the same stage as you pick them for eating, but for cucumbers and courgettes, you must leave the fruit on the plant for much longer than you would for a normal harvest. Scoop the seeds from the mature fruit into a large container of water, stir them vigorously to remove pieces of flesh, then rinse them in a sieve. The seeds of some fruits, particularly tomatoes and cucumbers, are often put through a natural fermentation process (*see page 96*) before cleaning, to destroy any seed-borne diseases that might be passed on to the next generation of plants.

Crops that produce seeds in pods, husks, capsules or any dry casing should be left on the plant until they are completely dry. If wet weather sets in, pull up whole plants and hang them in a dry airy place. Check seeding plants regularly – the seeds of some crops fall to the ground when they are ripe, so you need to harvest gradually over a long period to avoid losing them. The ripest seed umbels of a carrot plant, for example, may need covering with a paper bag in windy weather to collect fallen seed.

Your harvest will be a mixture of seed and 'chaff' - the pods and other debris, which should be separated and discarded before storage. Lightly roll or crush the mixture inside a bag or sack – the simple equivalent of a threshing machine – to separate the seeds from their cases. 'Winnowing' - separating the chaff from the seeds - was traditionally done by the wind, but a hair drier works fine. Shake small amounts of seed in a bowl until the debris collects at the top and then lightly blow it away. Alternatively, you can sieve the chaff from the seeds, or vice versa. Don't worry if your winnowing is not perfect!

Drying

It is essential that seeds are dried quickly and thoroughly before you store them, otherwise they may start to germinate or go mouldy. Small podded seeds that were harvested dry usually need minimal further treatment, but large seeds, and those harvested wet from fruit, need a longer drying time. A good air flow, rather than a high temperature, is the most important factor. Direct drying in the sun or oven can be damaging. Dry small quantities of seed in a large bowl on a shaded windowsill, stirring occasionally, or hang them in paper or netting bags in a warm airy spot. Label them with the variety name, origin, and date of harvest; good record keeping is invaluable when you are saving the seed of heritage varieties.

Storage

Seeds store best in a cool, dry, dark place where there is little temperature fluctuation. What seem like obvious places to put them – in the garden shed or on the kitchen shelf – are often the most unsuitable.

One effective way to create dry conditions for small quantities of seed is to keep them in paper packets in an airtight container with some silica gel crystals. Silica gel (available from most chemists) takes up water from the atmosphere inside the container and from the seeds, turning from blue to pink as it does so. You can then dry it in a very low oven until it turns back to blue, and put it back with the seeds. Use one teaspoonful of crystals per 30g (1oz) of seeds.

Store the jars of seeds in a cold place – a spare room or, ideally, in the refrigerator. Do not put them in the freezer unless you are confident that they are thoroughly dry. If seed moisture levels exceed 8%, their walls can be damaged as the water inside them freezes.

ABOVE: *In summer the Preservation Gardens at SSE are a patchwork of colour – here they are trialling varieties brought back from Eastern Europe.*

Most vegetable seeds will keep well for around three years if stored properly – but the time does vary from crop to crop; parsnip seeds, for example, are difficult to keep for longer than a year, whereas squash seeds can keep up to ten years. If you have more seed than you will use, give it away to friends and neighbours, or join a seed savers' network and pass it on. The more people that grow and appreciate heritage varieties, the more likely they are to survive.

SIMPLE SEED SAVING

TOMATOES

Tomatoes self-pollinate and are one of the easiest crops to save for seed; that is why we can find such a wide selection of heirloom varieties. Cross-pollination hardly ever occurs, except in some of the oldest varieties such as currant tomatoes (*Lycopersicon pimpinellifolium*). This should not be a problem unless you are growing several older varieties alongside one another.

Leave the fruits on the plants until they are really ripe, then cut them open and squeeze out the seeds and gel into a bowl. Leave the mixture in a warm place for several days, until a layer of mould covers the surface. It will smell very unpleasant, but it is worth putting up with this because the natural fermentation kills many seed-borne tomato diseases.

After 3 or 4 days scoop off the top fungal layer and use a sieve and clean water to wash the seeds. Tip them onto a plate or tray, and dry them in a warm place out of direct sunlight.

FRENCH BEANS

The numerous varieties of bush and climbing French beans are self-pollinating annual plants which are very easy to save for seed. Cross-pollination rarely occurs, but as a precaution, do not grow two varieties that you are saving for seed right alongside one another. Separate them by a few metres and/or grow another tall crop in between.

PLANT SELECTION:
When the plants are young, remove any with discoloured foliage or any other sign of disease. When some flowers and pods have formed, select about six plants with typical characteristics to save for seed. Mark them clearly so that no-one picks their pods to eat.

COLLECTING SEED:
Ideally, the pods should be left on the plant in the garden until they are completely dry. However, once they have turned from green to yellow/brown, you can safely pull up the whole plant and hang it upside down in a warm dry airy place – the seeds will continue to ripen. Do this if wet or frosty weather threatens.

CLEANING:
Pod small quantities by hand. Larger quantities should be placed in a sack, then tread all over it or beat it to split the pods and separate the seed. Remove the pods and other debris by hand or by blowing with a fan or hair drier.

DRYING:
Dry the seeds thoroughly in a warm airy place. Hang them in paper bags or thin hessian sacks, or lay them thinly on a drying tray made by stretching some fine mesh material across a wooden frame. Test whether the seeds are dry enough by hitting one or two with a hammer. They will shatter if dry, but will squash if further drying is necessary.

PUMPKINS AND WINTER SQUASHES

Pumpkins and winter squashes may belong to any one of several species, all of which look superficially very similar. They are annuals, differing botanically from most other vegetables in that they have separate male and female flowers on the same plant. The female flower has a distinct swelling at the base, whereas the male flower is on a long straight stem.

Bees love the flowers, and varieties of the same species readily cross-pollinate within a distance of about 500m (550yds). However, the blooms are large and easy to isolate and pollinate by hand.

PLANT SELECTION:
Growing six plants of any one variety is usually considered sufficient to maintain genetic diversity within the variety, although ideally you need twelve or more. However, this should not stop you from saving seed from fewer plants for a year or two if that is all you have room for. To pollinate a female flower on one plant, try to use male flowers from several other different plants.

HAND POLLINATION:
In early evening, find male and female flowers that are due to open the following morning. This is easy to determine with practice – the flowers begin to show a flush of yellow and may start to break open at the tip. Tape the tips of these blossoms shut with masking tape, or cover each of them with a piece of horticultural fleece, well secured where it meets the stem. In the morning, cut off the male flower, remove the tape or fleece and all the petals so that the anthers are exposed. Remove the tape or fleece from the female flower and open it gently; rub the anthers of the male flower onto the stigma in its centre. Re-tape or cover the female flower, and put a tag on the stem so that you can identify the fruit that you have pollinated when it is mature. Soon the flower will wilt and any cover can be removed. If pollination has been successful, the fruit will then start to swell.

COLLECTING SEED:
Harvest the fruits when they are fully mature, and then store them for a few weeks to allow the seeds to plump up. Cut the fruit open, and scrape out the seeds into a bowl.

CLEANING:
Add water to the seeds and rub them to remove any remaining pieces of flesh. Collect the seeds in a sieve.

DRYING:
Put the seeds to dry on a flat surface in a warm, dry and airy place. They are dry enough for storage when they break in half when you try to bend them.

PART

2

The Directory of
Heritage Vegetables

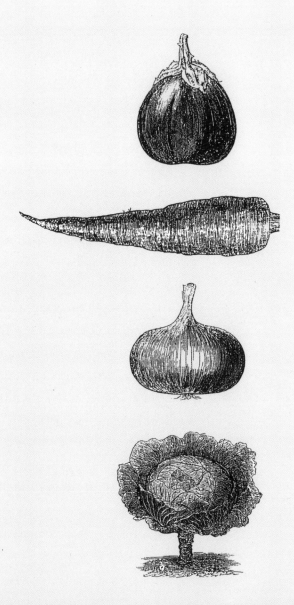

The **Directory** is not intended to be a definitive guide to heritage varieties. Its purpose is to point you in the right direction, to pick out a range of varieties that have stood the test of time and indicate the diversity of vegetables that are available for you to try. Many are not available from big commercial suppliers; you are more likely to find them in the lists of small specialist seed companies, often run by families or dedicated individuals who are working to ensure that a genuinely wide range of varieties is available to everyone.

Alternatively you could join a seed savers' network of people who grow and swap heritage seeds. Whichever course you choose, you will be rewarded with a garden full of interesting plants with fascinating histories, and above all superb flavours. Once you have begun to grow them, you will find that your vegetable plot can never be big enough.

The crop-by-crop descriptions in the **Directory** try to put each vegetable into a historical context and give some information about its cultivation. The exact origins of many vegetables are uncertain. There are tantalising glimpses of the past – for example, in records of Roman times, and in the works of botanists and gardeners such as John Evelyn in the 17th century and Philip Miller in the 18th century. But there are also frustrating gaps in our knowledge, and even experts often disagree on the times and places where crops were first cultivated. Nevertheless, looking at vegetables in this way helps to give you an insight into their characteristics and potential – where they are likely to thrive, and ways in which they might be useful.

Some of the varieties in the **Directory** are traditional garden favourites, popular enough to remain on the seed lists of the commercial companies for decades, but now threatened by modern hybrids. Others are family heirlooms or rediscovered local varieties; the European legislation has severely restricted the availability of such varieties, and most of those listed here have been sought out and maintained by seed savers' networks.

The inclusion of regional varieties from the whole of Northern Europe does not mean that British gardeners should seek out a remote Swedish landrace of pea, for example, or a carrot from a Swiss mountain village. It does show, however, that such local varieties exist, and that it is worth trying to find those that belong to your own area. These will have adapted over the years to your soil and climate, therefore they will have the best chance of doing well. They are also part of the culture. On the other hand, most vegetables are already much travelled, and we would have a very poor diet in Northern Europe if we had not, in the past, adopted plants from entirely foreign countries. Do not be afraid to try something new occasionally, and if you live in an area of short summers, an old Swedish pea could grow far better than the newest variety from a multinational seed company.

Sometimes varieties have come to the **Directory** from a seed saving network or small seed producer, with a personal recommendation and first-hand growing tips. Sometimes, however, descriptions have been taken from seed catalogues, and details are limited. We have tried to give some indication of cultivation requirements, climatic preferences and harvest times where these are available, but do not be down-hearted if your plants do not exactly match your expectations. Characteristics such as the time to maturity, size and even taste can vary from area to area, soil to soil, and season to season – and you have to bear in mind that plants of heritage varieties are not always identical.

More confusion can arise with synonyms, when two differently named varieties are said to be the same. Catalogues do not always agree on which varieties are synonyms; for example, some list the leek St Victor Blue as a synonym of Bleu de Solaise; others list the varieties separately. As we have seen, it is dangerous to assume that two varieties with similar appearance are identical. This is how the white-rot resistant onion Up-to-Date became lost to the market (*see page 65*). The exact genetic make-up of a variety cannot be determined without DNA testing, and where there is uncertainty it is better to give it the benefit of the doubt. In any case, if two varieties which were the same, but differently named, have been saved over a long period by different groups of people, in different climates, and under different conditions, they may have developed different genetic traits.

While this confusion may be irritating if you are used to growing the distinct and uniform hybrids sold through modern seed catalogues, it does not make heritage varieties any less valuable. It does, however, indicate the importance of keeping records when you grow them. Do try and pass the details on to your seed supplier or seed savers' network, as there is little information available about how many varieties perform under different growing conditions, and your experiences may help others.

All the varieties listed in the **Directory** were available in Northern Europe at the time of writing, either from a commercial seed company or seed saving network. Sources of supply for the individual varieties are not given – partly because this could bring attention to anyone that was selling an 'illegal' variety, but also because the **Directory** is not intended to be used in this way. Instead, the following section, the **Resources**, provides a list of small specialist seed suppliers – and you will almost certainly find more in your region if you seek them out. Their catalogues generally make fascinating and inspiring reading, and somewhere you should find just the varieties suited to you. When you contact small seed companies, remember that they have not got the resources of large commercial firms. Send return postage if you write, and be prepared to pay for catalogues.

Some of the main seed savers' networks in Northern Europe are also listed, and again there are likely to be more local groups if you look for them. You do not have to be an expert gardener or an experienced seed saver to join such a network. Most offer plenty of advice for newcomers, and many have open days and other events which you can join in, both to get to know the heritage varieties and to meet people that grow them. In your own garden, try starting with one or two easy crops, save the seeds and pass them on to friends, relatives and neighbours. Then you too will be helping to maintain our vegetable heritage, while at the same time enjoying the wonderful flavours of some of the traditional varieties.

Although gardening with heritage vegetables comes out of the past, it is vitally concerned with the present and the future, and the more people that are involved, the better it will be for all of us, and for the world that we live in. We hope that **Part Two** of this book will give you the information that you need to get started.

Contents

ARTICHOKES (GLOBE)
Cynara scolymus (Compositae)

Primitive forms of this vegetable were eaten by the Ancient Greeks and Romans. The globe artichoke is a handsome perennial plant, resembling a giant thistle, and it can look very attractive in the flower border. The plump green or purple-tinged immature flower buds are the edible parts.

Artichokes may be grown from seed, but these tend to be very variable; plants can also be propagated from offsets – rooted suckers taken from parent plants in spring.

A fertile well drained soil is necessary for successful cultivation. In areas with cold winters, protect plants by mounding earth round their base and covering the crowns with straw. If left unharvested, they produce attractive purple flowers, much loved by bees, and wonderful as dried ornaments. They will cross-pollinate with each other and with the closely related cardoons.

Gros vert de Laon / Paris artichoke
This used to be the preferred variety for French market gardeners in the late 1800s. Plants are vigorous and reasonably hardy, artichoke heads are large, broad and fleshy. If left to seed, the large heads form beautiful purple/pink flowers, very effective in the flower border or dried for decoration.

Green Globe
This is a traditional Northern European variety, now seen as a gourmet variety for its large 7-10 cm (3-4in) chokes and delicately flavoured outer leaves.

ARTICHOKES (JERUSALEM)
Helianthus tuberosus (Compositae)

Jerusalem artichokes are one of the few vegetables to originate in North America. The tubers were used by various Native American tribes, and were first taken to Europe by explorers in the 17th century. They are closely related to sunflowers. Some people believe their name is a corruption of 'girasole' the Italian for sunflower – certainly they have no connection with Jerusalem.

The plants are hardy perennials propagated by planting tubers or pieces of tuber any time from late winter to mid spring. They are extremely easy to grow, even in poor soils, but less easy to eradicate as every piece of unharvested tuber will resprout. Plants can reach 3m (10ft) tall, and are sometimes used as a quick windbreak or screen.

Chinese artichokes (*Stachys affinis*) belong to the *Labiateae* family, and are unrelated to Jerusalem artichokes despite some superficial similarities. They are sprawling plants with small ridged tubers, introduced into France in the late 19th century where they quickly became known as 'crosnes' after the place where they were first grown. The tubers have a delicate flavour, and can be used hot or in salads; they are easily propagated in the same way as Jerusalem artichokes.

Dwarf Sunray

This dwarf variety flowers freely, with small sunflower-like flowers, so is equally good in the flower border as in the vegetable patch. Like the plants, the tubers are small and squat with numerous side tubers, and some of them look remarkably like little animals or reptiles. Fortunately the skin is very tender, so these artichokes do not need peeling. They take longer to cook than other varieties – 30 minutes – and are delicious prepared with a white sauce.

Boston Red

The strong smoky flavour and floury texture of this old English variety make it the preferred variety for many chefs – it is the most popular artichoke in the US. The roots are large, knobbly, and purplish-skinned, peeling to creamy-white flesh; cook them for 20 minutes.

Fuseau

An old variety, introduced before 1920, uniform shaped long tubers are very smooth, almost knob-free, so very easy to prepare in the kitchen. Strong flavoured, these are highly recommended for soups.

Patate

Roots of this variety are very large, rounded and fairly smooth.

Waldboro Gold

This unusual variety has very thin yellow tubers with a distinctive flavour. The foliage is slightly different from other Jerusalem artichokes, so it is possible that this variety is a different species of *Helianthus*. The tubers spread rapidly, so give them space in your garden, but they are definitely worth trying as the flavour is superb – tubers take 15 minutes to cook.

ASPARAGUS
Asparagus officinalis (Liliaceae)

Asparagus is a native of Europe, found wild particularly in coastal regions, and cultivated since the times of the Ancient Greeks and Romans. It is a hardy perennial plant, grown for its delicious young shoots or spears which are harvested in spring. It flourishes on most soils, but must have good drainage. In gardens, asparagus is usually given its own permanent bed, and plants can remain productive for up to 20 years.

Normally asparagus has male and female flowers on separate plants, the female having red berries in autumn, which are easy to collect for seed. Many of the new hybrids now available have been bred to have all male plants. These produce more spears of a good size and appearance for marketing, but old open-pollinated varieties still give satisfactory yields for gardeners and have a stronger asparagus flavour.

You can start asparagus plants from seed, buy young plants, or buy 'crowns' (one- or two-year-old roots). Sow seed in a seed bed and allow to grow on for one season, then the following spring select the largest and best crowns for planting out in your permanent asparagus bed. Spears should not be harvested until the second spring after planting.

Connover's Colossal

New in 1872, this huge asparagus is an early and
heavy cropper, an excellent old standard variety.
Particularly recommended for light and sandy soils.

Hâtive d'Argenteuil

Probably the best known asparagus, this was the
favourite variety for market gardeners in northern
France a century ago. Thick shoots have slightly
pointed purplish tips. The flavour is superb.

AUBERGINES
Solanum melongena (Solanaceae)

Aubergines are native to tropical Asia, and
were probably introduced to Southern
Europe by the Arabs as early as the 7th
century, thereafter becoming a common
ingredient in Mediterranean and Greek
cooking. They are perennials, but are grown
as annuals in cool climates.

The aubergines you see in supermarkets
and greengrocers are usually large purple egg-
shaped fruits, but there are many other
varieties which have fruits in different shapes
and colours. The American name 'egg plant'
probably came from the small white fruit of
an early type cultivated in Northern Europe.

Aubergines need a fertile soil, and warm
and humid conditions – ideally temperatures
should be over 18°C (64°F). To get good
crops in cool climates they usually need starting off with heat in spring and planting out in
a glasshouse or polytunnel. This is especially
necessary if you want fruit mature enough to
save for seed. The flowers self-pollinate, but
some crossing is likely to occur if different
varieties are grown together.

Early Long Purple

The classic long deep purple fruit, this is the best
aubergine for short summer areas. Grown in Europe
since the late 19th century, this variety has excellent
flavour and is delicious sliced and fried. Remove small
fruits to leave no more than six per plant.

Blanche Ronde à oeuf

This old-fashioned early variety produces round white
fruits which should be picked when they are the size
of an egg. They taste rather like mushrooms.

Violette di Firenze

Traditional variety with large heavy round fruits, purple
with a pale blush at the stalk end. Each plant will
produce 8 to 10 fruits.

BROAD BEANS
Vicia faba (Leguminosae)

Before travellers brought French and runner beans back from the Americas, broad beans were the only type grown in Europe. They have been cultivated here since prehistoric times, and several very old landraces can still be found. Broad beans are grown mostly for the freshly shelled beans, but the whole pods can be eaten if picked very young, and some people also eat the young leaf tips as greens. The beans can also be dried.

The plants need fertile moist soil. They are annuals, but unlike French and runner beans, they will tolerate some frost. In mild regions they can be sown in autumn for picking in early summer the following year; otherwise sow them in early spring. Some varieties are more hardy than others. The plants can vary in height from 45cm (1^1/$_2$ft) to 2m (6^1/$_2$ft) depending on variety, and they also differ in the size and colour of their seeds. Green-seeded varieties are often considered the most tender for eating fresh.

The flowers self-pollinate, but bees can also cause cross-pollination, so isolation is necessary for seed saving if there are other varieties growing nearby.

Crimson-flowered Broad Bean

Known to have been grown at the end of the 18th century, crimson-flowered broad beans are attractive enough to be used as ornamentals in the flower border. Pods, which remain pointing upwards when mature, are small but tightly packed with tasty bright green beans. This variety is a favourite heritage variety in the UK, growing from seeds donated to the Heritage Seed Library in 1978 by an elderly lady whose father had been given the seeds when he was a boy, a century earlier.

Martock

These small brown-seeded beans date right back to medieval times, long preserved in the UK in the Bishop of Bath and Wells' kitchen garden from where they were once offered to people in exchange for a donation towards repair of Wells Cathedral! Martock is probably very similar to the beans that were the staple diet of many North European medieval villagers.

Red Epicure

Fine quality long pods are produced by this variety, with deep chestnut-crimson seeds. Although the colour fades in cooking, it still retains a superb flavour.

Windsor – Green and White Windsor

Vigorous and productive, Windsors have long broad pods that mature later than many other varieties, but have excellent flavour. White Windsors were praised in a catalogue in 1729. The seeds of Green Windsors are bright green, whether fresh or dried. These beans will not survive the winter in very frosty areas.

Aquadulce / Aquadulce Claudia

One of the most popular British heritage varieties, these hardy beans are good for early spring or autumn sowing for an early crop. Medium to long pods contain white beans which are ideal for freezing. **Aquadulce** came to Northern Europe from Spain in the 1850s.

Bohusläns Delikatess

One of a number of old local Swedish varieties of broad bean, this one from Bohuslån is easy to grow and high yielding. It is 1m (3 ft) tall, and has light green seeds.

Swedish Purple

An old Swedish variety with dark purple seeds. Taken to the US by Swedish settlers and saved as an heirloom, it has recently been returned to the Swedish seedsaving group SESAM.

FRENCH BEANS & RUNNER BEANS
Phaseolus vulgaris & Phaseolus coccineus (Leguminosae)

French and runner beans originated in Central and South America where they have been cultivated since ancient times. They are relatively new to Europe, only arriving after Columbus crossed the Atlantic at the end of the 15th century.

French beans can be either dwarf (bush) habit, or climbing (sometimes called pole beans). Some are grown to be eaten as whole green pods (snap beans), in others the pods are allowed to become more mature and the beans are then podded and eaten fresh. Beans for drying are harvested when the pods are fully mature and dry. Many of the traditional varieties are multi-purpose, and are good eaten shelled fresh, as snap or as dry beans.

French beans are fast-growing annuals. They need a warm soil (over 12⁰C, 53⁰F) for germination and they are frost tender. In cool climates, sow seeds indoors in late spring and plant them out when all danger of frost has passed. Alternatively, sow bush varieties under cloches or frames for an early crop. The flowers self-pollinate and crossing is relatively rare, but do not grow two varieties for seed next to one another.

French beans vary considerably in colour and in the shape of their pods and seeds; since seed saving is easy, many heritage varieties can still be found.

The same is true of runner beans. Varieties of the traditional scarlet runners can be traced back to the Hopi Indians in North America. When the beans were first introduced into Europe, they were often grown for their flowers rather than their pods. However, they quickly became popular as a vegetable in the UK, and remain so today. In Britain they are almost always grown for the immature green or 'snap' beans, but in other countries the shelled fresh beans or dried beans are also popular.

Runner beans are perennials, but are usually grown as annuals – although it is possible to overwinter their fleshy roots in a frost-free place. Most varieties are tall, climbing to around 3m (10ft), but there are a few modern dwarf varieties. Flowers are usually red or white, the white-flowered varieties have white seeds.

Runner beans will self-pollinate, but there can also be considerable crossing between varieties, so isolation may be necessary to get pure seed. The flowers may not set and form pods unless they are shaken (normally by insects or the wind), and they may also fail to set at high temperatures – over 32°C (90°F).

CLIMBING FRENCH BEANS

Purple Giant
A strong-growing productive bean. Attractive purple pods are easy to spot among the dark green foliage. Though these beans are best eaten fresh, the brown seeds are also very good dried.

Veitch's Climbing
This variety is a good prolific cropper covered in straight long flat pods all over the bush. It does not grow well in cool damp conditions but produces best in a warm summer; slender pods are best eaten green.

Trail of Tears /Cherokee Trail of Tears
This bean was carried by Cherokee Indians on their forced repatriation in the 1830s, the march that became known as the Trail of Tears (*see page 53*). Lavender flowers appear on highly productive vines which produce slender purple pods with small black seeds, traditionally dried for winter use.

Coco Bicolour
A very prolific and historic French bean with white beans splashed pink. A very early crop of delicious stringless pods is produced in which beans develop rapidly. This variety is excellent for fresh eating, or for drying. It is particularly good at high altitudes.

Caseknife
Grown since 1820, this vigorous climber produces masses of stringless pale green pods. Best eaten whole, the beans can also be used dried.

Golden Butter / Mont d'Or
Grown since the 1870s, this productive early variety produces medium-sized fine-textured golden pods. Young beans are stringless and tasty.

DWARF/BUSH FRENCH BEANS

Hutterite Soup
Developed in the early 19th century by the Hutterite religious communities of North America, this is a great soup variety as the beans don't need any pre-soaking. Pale lemon-yellow beans with a black eye cook to a smooth creamy consistency, with delicious flavour.

Jacob's Cattle
This very old variety is reliably early and good for short-season areas. Beans are very beautiful, blotched red, purple and brown like Jacob's cattle in the Biblical story, usually eaten dried rather than fresh.

Early Warwick
Grown in England since the 1880s, this variety used to be greatly prized for its reliable early heavy production of beans for drying. Dry beans are mottled pink and maroon, and pods are also very good if picked and eaten young.

Chevrier Vert

This is a classic flageolet bean, originally developed from the traditional Green Flageolet by a French market gardener called Chevrier. Tasty and tender green-white French beans are perfect for many dishes.

Swedish Brown

Well adapted for cool climates, this old variety has orange-brown beans with excellent flavour for soups and salads.

Black Valentine

This very old heritage variety is a good choice for early planting Straight, slender dark green pods grow to 20cm (8 in), and are stringless at all stages.

Gotländsk Spräcklig

A Swedish drying bean from the island of Gotland. The seeds are large pink/white or red/white speckled. They have a high content of oxalic acid which is why they turn dark with age. Pods are flat and fairly short, and can be eaten green when young.

Gotländsk Vax

Another local Swedish variety from the island of Gotland. It has long yellow waxy pods and is relatively high yielding even in a cold climate.

RUNNER BEANS

Painted Lady

The Royal Horticultural Society *Dictionary of Plants* lists four varieties of runner beans introduced to the UK in 1633. Painted Lady was one of these. It has red and white flowers, followed by a good crop of medium-length delicately flavoured green beans.

Czar

Flowers are white, and long tender pods contain white seeds (*see page 69*). These beans are very tasty cooked and eaten fresh, but if they are left to dry you will get a good crop of buttery beans.

Lobengula

This black-seeded runner bean has fleshy pods with a very good flavour. Very attractive and uniform, these beans are often grown as exhibition beans, and have been winning at shows in the UK for the past 80 years.

Scarlet Emperor / Scarlet Runner

Popular since the 1890s, red-flowered plants reliably produce good crops of fairly uniform pods, with very good flavour.

Sunset

Hailing from the US, these are one of the best varieties for short-season areas, and have beautiful pink-orange flowers on strong vines. They are now only obtainable in Europe through seed saving organisations.

LABLAB BEANS / HYACINTH BEANS
Dolichos lablab (Leguminosae)

These beans have been grown for centuries in China, where they are very prolific. They are attractive climbing plants with flat slightly curved pods which are generally picked and used young. There are purple and green forms. In Northern Europe the purple forms are becoming popular for their ornamental foliage and clusters of purple flowers, but they will form edible pods, especially if grown in a glasshouse or polytunnel. Like French and runner beans when they first arrived in Europe, they may need to become adapted to cooler days and different daylengths to give a good crop.

No named varieties are available.

YARD LONG BEAN / ASPARAGUS BEAN
Dolichos sesquipedalis (Leguminosae)

The yard long bean probably originated in China or was introduced there in prehistoric times. In Europe it has recently been promoted as a novelty although it is not new – in the 1880s Vilmorin mentions its cultivation in the South of France, especially Provence. Although the beans may not reach a yard (1m) long in cool climates, they usually grow to around half that length if grown in a polytunnel. Despite their length, it is best to pick the green beans when around 30cm (12in) long, before they toughen.

There are forms with pale green, dark green or purple pods, but named varieties are not generally listed.

No named varieties are available.

BEETROOT
Beta vulgaris (Chenopodiaceae)

Beetroot and the closely related chards and fodder beets were developed from wild beets, native to North Africa and the coastal areas of Southern Europe. The Romans are said to have introduced them to Northern Europe, where they became well adapted to the cool climate. Many traditional recipes for using beetroot come from Germany, Scandinavia and Eastern Europe.

The roots can be various shapes – round, flat or long-rooted, depending on variety – and although their flesh is normally a deep reddish purple, there are yellow and white forms. Beetroot leaves are also edible, used like chard or spinach beet, or young in salads.

A rich light soil is the best for growing beetroot, not one that has been freshly manured. The plants are biennial, but do not stand hard winter frosts, and must be lifted and stored in late autumn in cool climates. Sow them in mid to late spring for roots that can be pulled young for eating fresh, and in early summer for larger roots for winter storage. Beetroot sown too early when the weather is still cold are likely to bolt later in the season.

All varieties of beetroot will cross-pollinate with each other beetroot, and also with closely-related chard and spinach beet.

Cook's Delight
This fast-growing tankard-shaped beetroot has very dark red leaves which are ornamental enough to grow in a flower border. The roots are best picked small and young for fresh eating, but they store very well, retaining a good flavour if you leave them to mature.

Barbietola di Choggia
It is not known when this variety was introduced to Northern Europe from its original home in Italy, but it has been available for many decades. This is a highly attractive beetroot, with cut rings alternating red and white, perfect for salads. Unfortunately the rings disappear on cooking, leaving the whole vegetable a slightly insipid pink, but the flavour is very good.

Bulls Blood
This is probably the only decorative leaved Victorian variety surviving, usually grown nowadays for its spectacular reddish purple leaves which look very attractive grown among shrubs and perennials. The flavour of the medium-sized spherical roots is best when young, they become tough with age.

Egyptian Turnip-rooted
The smooth slightly flat roots of this early variety have beautifully coloured deep red flesh and a good flavour. This is the best variety for shallow soils, and also for smaller gardens as it does not develop a large top and so can be grown closer together than other old-fashioned beets.

Dorée

This is a very old golden variety, with exceptionally sweet flavour and smooth texture. Delicious cooked, or grated in salads, this is also one of the best varieties for pickling.

Rouge Crapaudine

This is probably the oldest variety we know, distinguishable from others by its almost black skin which is pocked with cracks and crevices, and its long – often misshapen – roots. The flesh is red and very sweet and firm. This beetroot crops late; sow in May to harvest in late autumn or early winter.

Albina Vereduna / Snow White

This unusual variety has pale skin and ice-white flesh. The roots are extremely sweet but delicately flavoured, and the curled leaves are delicious as cooked greens or as salad ingredients when picked young – they are also very high in Vitamin C.

BROCCOLI
Brassica oleracea var *Italica (Cruciferae)*

Sprouting broccoli was derived from the wild cabbage (*Brassica oleracea*) by selecting for tender young flowering shoots. In broccoli these are formed in a cluster at the top of the plant and as numerous side shoots. The vegetable was developed in Italy, and probably introduced into Northern Europe around the 17th century, when it was sometimes called Italian asparagus.

Purple and white forms of sprouting broccoli are large biennial plants, growing up to 90cm (3ft) in height and spread. They are sown in late spring and will overwinter unless the weather is very severe, giving a useful crop the following spring. The purple forms are considered hardier than the white. Only a small number of open-pollinated varieties are available, differing mainly in their cropping period, and in the last few years F1 hybrids have been introduced.

Calabrese, or green sprouting broccoli varieties are generally smaller and faster growing than purple and white broccoli, but they are not so hardy. They can be sown from spring to early summer and usually crop about $2^1/_2$ months later, depending on variety. Most modern varieties of calabrese are F1 hybrids, bred to produce large heads all at one time for the supermarket and for freezing.

Broccoli will cross with cabbage and other similar brassicas, and it is not simple to save for seed (*see Chapter 5, pages 90-97*).

Purple Sprouting

The generic name for many unnamed varieties of sprouting broccoli. There are early and late selections to be harvested in early or late spring. **Purple Sprouting** is very hardy and easy to grow and produces masses of small purple sprouts (flower heads) from early spring.

White Sprouting

Carter's Seeds introduced this to the UK as 'new' in 1862. Slightly less hardy and more delicately flavoured than its purple equivalent, it produces delicious shoots like miniature cauliflowers.

Nine Star Perennial

Whereas most broccolis will need to be resown every year, this variety will keep on bearing pure white shoots for as long as five years. If your garden is in a cold place, mulch the broccoli well over the winter.

De Cicco / Ramoso

This old Italian variety of calabrese can be grown for spring or autumn cropping. Following the main central head, a large number of variable sized side shoots will appear, producing delicious and tender sprouts.

Romanesco

Another old Italian variety which has become increasingly popular in the last couple of years. Pale green heads can be up to 15cm (6in) across, with curds arranged in a spiralling pattern like a minaret (*see page 25*). It has a very soft texture and delicious flavour. A late autumn harvesting variety, sow in May to harvest in October.

BRUSSELS SPROUTS
Brassica oleracea var *gemnifera (Cruciferae)*

The wild cabbage is also the ancestor of Brussels sprouts, developed relatively recently in Belgium. These vegetables did not become well known in the UK or France until the 19th century. They are reasonably hardy biennial plants that make a good winter crop in cool climates, as long as the winters are not too severe. The tight 'sprouts' which form up the stem are traditionally eaten steamed or boiled, but they are also very tasty when sliced and stir-fried.

Brussels sprouts need well drained moisture-retentive soil, as long as it has not been recently manured. Seed is usually sown in a seed bed in mid spring and plants put out in early summer. To ensure tight sprouts, the soil must be firm so that the plants do not rock or topple over.

Using different varieties and/or sowing times, it is possible to harvest sprouts from early autumn until well into the following spring. Traditional open-pollinated varieties have largely been replaced by F1 hybrids which give a crop of tighter sprouts, uniformly distributed up the stem. Seed saving is not easy (*see Chapter 5, pages 90-97*), and heirloom varieties are hard to find.

Wroxton

Introduced in 1895 as one of the first 'dwarf' varieties, although, growing to 90–120 cm (3–4ft) it is not dwarf by modern standards. It produces a crop of large sprouts, which can be obtained throughout winter and into spring by making two successive sowings, one in early March, and one in mid April.

Bedford Winter Harvest

Many strains of Brussels sprouts were developed in the 19th century in Bedfordshire in England, this is one that is still available. It is extremely hardy, producing dark green sprouts on very strong plants, from October to February.

Evesham Special

Ideal for growing in exposed conditions, this popular old market garden variety is a good reliable producer with firm, early crops. The sprouts are large and tasty, growing on medium-sized stocky plants.

Rubine / Rubine Red

A highly attractive example of the red type available since early this century. Very ornamental, this variety is a reliable producer and extremely frost-hardy.

De Rosny

This is probably the classic French variety. Firm dark green sprouts are produced throughout the winter months on strong hardy plants.

CABBAGES
Brassica oleracea var *capitata (Cruciferae)*

Cabbages are one of the oldest known of the green vegetables. Types of cabbage were cultivated by the Celts and later by the Romans, although these probably had relatively loose leaves compared to the solid-headed cabbages we grow today.

In cool climates where winters are not too severe, cabbages can be harvested fresh all year round, and varieties are generally classified according to the season. Those picked in summer and autumn are sown in succession from early spring to early summer. Winter cabbages are sown in late spring. Spring cabbages are sown in mid to late summer and are overwintered as small plants which heart up early the following spring. However, old varieties do not always fit neatly into these categories. Summer and autumn cabbages include the red cabbages, which have a long history of cultivation in Europe. In *The Vegetable Garden* in 1885 Vilmorin describes them as being eaten raw in salads or shredded and pickled in vinegar. Winter cabbages include the very hardy crinkly leaved Savoy types. Most traditional spring cabbage varieties have conical heads. These are the trickiest to grow; they can easily be killed in severe winters, or, if conditions are not right, tend to bolt without hearting up in the spring.

Cabbages need a fertile, well drained and moisture-retentive soil – ideally the ground should have been manured the autumn before planting. They are biennial plants, and saving seed is not simple (*see Chapter 5, pages 90-97*). Although there are still many open-pollinated cabbages available, most commercial growers and a lot of gardeners now use the more predictable modern hybrids, and heritage varieties are not easy to find.

SPRING CABBAGES

April

Suttons Seeds catalogue of 1897 described this variety as the earliest of all spring cabbages. It forms tasty dwarf compact hearts very early in spring, and is very slow to bolt.

Early Jersey Wakefield

Originally an American variety called Early Heart-shaped, this has been in cultivation since 1726. It deserves to be more widely grown today as 1–1.5kg (2–3lb) heads are of a superb eating quality and stand and store well without splitting. Very firm compact heads are dark waxy green and shaped like an upside down cone. Although traditionally used as a spring cabbage, **Early Jersey Wakefield** can also be sown in March or April for cutting in August and September.

Ellams Early Dwarf

Grown since the 1880s, this is another dwarf variety that is slow to bolt and reliably produces very tight compact hearts.

Delaway

This dark green spring cabbage comes from Northern Ireland. It is unusual as it can be used as a cut-and-come-again variety – if the leaves are picked individually they will regrow like spinach. This variety was traditionally used in the much loved Northern Irish dish of bacon and cabbage, and was also the favourite variety for making Colcannon, where potatoes and cabbage are mashed together.

SUMMER AND AUTUMN CABBAGES

Shetland

Originally the only variety grown in the Shetland Isles, off Northern Scotland, this cabbage has a large rounded head which is very dense and sometimes has purple tinged leaves. It is very hardy, and well flavoured.

Best of All

Sow this variety in late spring for harvesting in the late autumn. It is easy to grow, withstanding cold or heat to produce a solid head with dark green crinkled leaves. Flavour and texture are superb.

Chou de Saint-Saëns

This enormous cabbage has been cultivated since the last century by generations of growers at Saint-Saëns in Northern France. It has grey-green leaves with pink veining and a striking pointed head. It can have a spread of over 1.4m (4ft) and weigh over 20kg (40lb). Young plants are overwintered for setting out the following spring and the cabbages are ready for harvesting in the autumn.

Premstättner Kraut

A traditional commercial white cabbage variety which is still available in Austria. It is early, forms a large head, and does not seem to be bothered as much by the cabbage moth as other varieties. It can be cooked fresh, or soured as sauerkraut.

WINTER CABBAGES

Milan de Pontoise / Hiver de Pontoise

An early winter Savoy cabbage, one of the many vegetable varieties developed in the Pont Oise area of Northern France in the 19th century, and market gardeners in the area still save their own heritage strains. This forms a very dense head with markedly crinkle-edged leaves. Extremely hardy, it is easy to grow in most climates.

Gros de Vertus

A very large solid headed Savoy variety for autumn through winter harvest. The head is thick, compact, round with a slightly flattened top. Leaves are usually purplish tinged with slightly crinkled edges.

Winnigstadt

This dwarf cabbage was described as a new variety in 1859. It produces very broad-based conical heads with dense compact hearts. Wait until the cabbages are mature before harvesting, then the leaves will be tender and sweet.

RED CABBAGES

Red Drumhead

Probably identical to the **Choux Rouge Gros** mentioned in Vilmorin's *The Vegetable Garden* in 1885, this variety has been grown since 1835. It has a particularly good flavour, excellent raw or cooked. Sow in February–April for autumn harvest.

Langedijker Bewaar / Langedijk Red Late

This is one of the best storage varieties; it doesn't lose flavour even if stored for several months after harvesting in September. Plants are strong and reliable producers of heavy dense cabbages.

Couve Tronchuda / Portuguese / Sea Kale Cabbage

This old Portuguese variety is an essential ingredient in the traditional *Caldo Verde* soup. It resembles the kale-like ancestral wild cabbage, with a large open hearted head that can grow to more than $2/3$m (2ft) across. Very sweet and thick midribs can be cooked separately from the leaves like chard, and the leaves are also very tender. Although it can withstand some frost, which improves the flavour, this is best grown as a half-hardy annual; it tolerates heat better than most other cabbages.

CARDOONS
Cynara cardunculus (Compositae)

Like the globe artichokes to which they are closely related, cardoons are large thistle–like plants native to Mediterranean regions. They are grown for their leaf stalks and midribs, which are blanched and used in salads, soups and stews. Cardoons were popular in England and France at the end of the 19th century, but are rarely grown in Northern Europe today, either by gardeners or commercial growers. However, they are still used in traditional dishes in Southern France, Spain and Italy.

Cardoons are grown from seed, sown in mid to late spring. They are vigorous plants, growing to a height of around 1.5m (5ft) with abundant foliage, and need a rich moisture-retentive soil. In autumn when they are fully grown, the stalks are blanched by tying the leaves together and wrapping the plant with cardboard packed in with straw. Cardoons will not stand hard frosts, and should be dug up and stored before severe weather sets in. Old varieties of cardoon differed in size, and in the rib width. However, named varieties are rarely listed today.

Gigante di Romagna

This is probably one of the original cardoon varieties popular in England in the 17th century. It is a stunning tall decorative plant for the vegetable or flower garden, growing to 2.5m (8ft) or more, with beautiful silver-grey architectural leaves.

Rouge d'Alger

Popular in France in the last century, this is probably the best variety for an edible landscape as it is extremely decorative, with red edged leaves, and a red tinge to the stalks. It grows to about 2m (6ft).

CARROTS
Daucus carota (Umbelliferae)

Although some wild carrots are native to Europe, cultivated carrots are said to have originated in Afghanistan. Records dating back to the Middle Ages describe purple, red and white carrots; orange varieties were developed in Holland and France much later.

Carrots grow best on light well drained soils. They should be sown directly outside from mid spring to mid summer, and harvested throughout the summer and autumn. In mild climates they can be left to overwinter in the ground, mulched with straw for protection; otherwise they should be lifted and stored before severe weather sets in. Biennials, the flowers do not appear until the second season, and these are pollinated by insects, so isolate varieties if you are saving seed (*see Chapter 5, pages 90-97*).

Carrot varieties differ greatly in size, shape, and in the time to maturity. Small round or stump-rooted carrots are best for quick fresh crops, or on heavy soils. Larger long-rooted varieties store best.

White Belgium
The pure white roots of this old European variety are deliciously mild, quite different from most other varieties, and useful for those people who can't tolerate carotene. In the 1800s this was used as animal fodder, and was the preferred crop for summer horse feed in France, but it is also a very tasty variety for the table. **White Belgium** is extremely productive, even on poorer soils, but plants are not hardy, so dig your carrots up before frost.

Guerande / Oxheart
Unusual club-shaped deep orange roots are short and very thick – 15cm (6in) long and about 12cm (5in) diameter – good eaten fresh or stored. These are definitely worth growing for their appearance as well as taste.

St Valery / Long Red Surrey
This long orange tapered type was popular in the 1880s but is now rare. It has long 23cm (10in) roots that are very sweet and tender with a fine texture and a distinctive yellow core. For best results grow this variety in deep rich soil.

Jaune du Doubs
This attractive carrot from France has cylindrical yellow roots with very sweet sugary flesh. Originally viewed as a fodder crop, it is an excellent stew or soup carrot, which stores well over winter and can be grown in fairly shallow soils.

James Scarlet Intermediate
This is a very good maincrop carrot with fairly uniform orange tapered roots of about 12cm (5in). It can be pulled young or lifted in October for winter storage.

London Market
A traditional variety with very wide stumpy roots which are a rich dark red colour. They are sweet and juicy, good raw or cooked.

Violet Carrot
This old variety has a thick squat cone-shaped root with a violet skin and red flesh. It is very hardy and quick to mature, and could do well in dry areas or harsh conditions.

CAULIFLOWERS
Brassica oleracea var *botrytis (Cruciferae)*

Cauliflowers are another brassica with wild cabbage in their ancestry. The head which we eat is a mass of partially developed flower buds. They were supposedly first cultivated about 2000 years ago in Eastern Mediterranean areas, arriving in Southern Europe in the 14th century, and then adapted and popularised in the cooler climates of mid and northern Europe. By the 16th century they were widely grown and had become well acclimatised to cooler climates, although the plants probably had much smaller heads than modern varieties.

Cauliflowers are usually classified according to the time that they produce heads for harvesting. Winter-heading varieties can only be grown in frost-free areas, but the relatively hardy spring-heading cauliflowers can be overwintered where the weather is not severe. The coastal areas of Southwest Britain and Northwest France are traditionally important cauliflower producing areas.

Cauliflowers are not the easiest vegetables to grow. They are sown from early spring to early summer, depending on variety, and need a deep, fertile, moisture-retentive soil. If they receive any check to growth, such as lack of water or nutrients, or an unexpected cold period, they may produce tiny premature heads. The curds of cauliflower can be protected from light frosts or hot sun by wrapping the outer leaves over the head.

Veitch's Self-protecting

Introduced in the 1870s, this strong-growing variety crops in October, producing firm heads with a good white colour. Hardy and reliable, it will stand into late November without spoiling.

St George

This reliable old variety produces solid white heads with tight curds, to be harvested in April or May from a late May sowing the previous year.

Snow's Winter White

Easier to grow than spring varieties, this is a valuable and popular mid-winter cauliflower. In 1843 a seedsman wrote: "If one could depend on getting this sort true, no other would be needed, as it is so thoroughly self-protecting".

Purple Cape

Popular in most of Europe in the 1830s, this beautiful purple-headed variety is hardy, cropping in February and March. The curd turns green when cooked; it has excellent flavour.

CELERY & CELERIAC
Apium graveolens vars. *dulce & rapaceum (Umbelliferae)*

Wild celery is native to Asia and much of Europe, flourishing in damp marshy areas. It was used as a medicinal plant in early times, but the thick-stemmed plant we know today is a relatively recent crop, developed by the French and Italians in the late 15th and 16th centuries. Celeriac is closely related to celery, but the base of the stem has been developed into a swollen 'root'. Seeds of celeriac were said to have reached Europe from Alexandria in the 18th century. Although less popular than celery, it is well worth growing, delicious in soups and stews, or mashed with potato, or grated raw in salad.

Traditional celery varieties must be blanched: they should be planted in a trench and earthed up, or heavy paper collars wrapped around them to exclude light. More recently, yellow and green self-blanching celeries have been developed which are easier to grow but with a less distinctive flavour.

All celeries need fertile soil and plenty of moisture. Both seeds and young plants need temperatures around 10°C (50°F), so they are usually sown under protection and planted out. Exposure to prolonged cold periods is liable to cause bolting later in the season. Self-blanching celery is harvested from sum-mer until the first frosts, traditional 'trench' celery can be left in the ground for longer, and pink and red-tinged varieties are said to be the hardiest.

Celeriac needs similar soil and temperature conditions. In mild areas it can be left in the ground to overwinter if mulched with straw.

Celery and celeriac are biennials, pollinated by insects. Varieties of celery will cross with each other and with celeriac, and vice-versa.

CELERY

Giant Red
A traditional English variety, developed in the 1870s. Compact heads are very thick, up to 30cm (12in) in girth, 60cm (2ft) tall, with red stalks and bright green leaves. This variety needs blanching; it is very aromatic, perfect for soups and all sorts of flavouring. The red stalks keep their colour when cooked, and this variety gives high yields of spicy celery seed.

Golden Self-Blanching
An old French variety. Tender, stringless and delicately flavoured, it is disease-resistant and easy to grow from seed. Compact plants have thick, tender, stringless stalks, blanching to yellow, and good thick hearts.

Giant Pink / Clayworth's Prize Pink
This old-fashioned British variety produces sturdy plants with crisp stalks tinged with pink. It blanches quickly and easily and has a strong flavour, even when plants are immature.

Solid White
The stems of this old variety are very crisp, white and solid with a fantastic flavour. It is probably the best of all varieties for eating raw, and used to be popular for exhibition use as it looks so striking. Many modern varieties are descended from this original parent.

CELERIAC

Giant Prague

The best of the older types of celeriac, first mentioned in 1870; thick white almost spherical roots are evenly shaped, 5–10cm (2–4in) diameter with few side rootlets. This is excellent in stews or soups, grated, or steamed and sliced cold in winter salads. It is delicious mashed with potato.

Snow White

This early variety has knobbly globe-shaped roots about 12cm (5in) diameter. They are very white, with a delicious nutty flavour, but more difficult to prepare than smoother varieties.

CHICORY
Cichorium intybus (Compositae)

Wild chicory is native to Europe and Western Asia, and the plant has a long history of cultivation. Classical Roman writers mention its use both as a cooked vegetable and as a salad leaf, and it was widely used as a medicinal plant. Many traditional chicories available today originate in Italy, where a wide range are still cultivated. Chicories are mostly perennial plants, but are usually grown as annuals. There are several distinct kinds, some used for their leaves and some for their roots.

Red-leaved chicories (Radicchio) and green-leaved chicories are usually used as salad plants, providing a slightly bitter flavour. They are sown from late spring onwards, and harvested in late summer and early autumn. Some varieties are very hardy and will over-winter where frosts are not too severe, providing a valuable source of fresh leaves in early spring. Chicories have varied leaf shapes, from smooth round types to those that are long and jagged like dandelions, and attractive red chicory varieties range from those with deep red leaves, to those with a pink tinge.

Some chicory varieties can be forced in the dark to produce sweeter pale shoots. Roots are usually lifted and stored in autumn, and brought into growth in gentle heat, up to 10°C (50°F), in a root cellar or under a flower pot in a glasshouse. The large-rooted Witloof chicories are usually forced in this way, producing tight white buds or 'chicons' for salads or cooking. Some say this method was discovered when a Belgian farmer threw some roots into a warm dark stable, although others attribute the idea to the head of the Brussels Botanical Garden!

In their second season chicories produce tall flower spikes covered with beautiful clear blue flowers. They are pollinated by insects, and can cross with other chicories and with endive if these are flowering within a few hundred metres of each other.

RED-LEAVED CHICORY / RADICCHIO

Variegata de Castelfranco

Developed in the 18th century in the Castelfranco region of Northern Italy, this very decorative variety has red blotched leaves and forms a loose inner head of red and white in autumn. This is a delicious winter salad ingredient, which can be used as a cutting or forcing variety.

Rossa di Verona / Red Verona

Use this very adaptable variety as a cutting or forcing chicory: round tight heads of magenta-red leaves with white ribs are formed in early winter after the first green leaves are cut back in autumn. Add sparingly to salads (it has a sharp tangy flavour) or brush with oil and grill. If you cut **Rossa di Verona** back in autumn, and protect it over the winter, second growth produces fine heads in spring with a very solid red and white heart.

GREEN-LEAVED CHICORY

Grumolo Verde

This fine green variety from Piedmont is very winter hardy. The plants form tight rosettes of tender green leaves which can be picked until late summer, then plants are left to be cut again in spring.

Catalogne à Punterelle

This is a very old cutting chicory, the traditional salad choice. To enjoy the leaves at their most tender, soak them for an hour in water before adding to salads.

Barbe de Capuchin / Monk's Beard

A cultivated form of the wild chicory, which has jagged leaves similar to a dandelion. The young leaves can be eaten green in summer as a cut-and-come-again crop. The roots of the mature plants are traditionally forced and blanched to produce the tender *barbes de capuchin* (literally 'monks' beards'), described in 1885 by Vilmorin as a "highly esteemed vegetable".

Witloof Chicory

This is the chicory traditionally used in Northern Europe to force tender young white buds or chicons for winter and early spring use. Sowing seed in early summer will produce vigorous plants with long green leaves, which should be left growing until late autumn. The large roots are then lifted and stored for forcing as required. Named varieties of Witloof chicory are rarely listed, although some F1 hybrids have recently been introduced.

ROOT CHICORY

Magdeburg

Grown for its large roots, which are dried, roasted, and ground for a coffee substitute or additive. Vitamin-rich leaves are delicious for flavouring soups and salads. The practice of using chicory for coffee dates from the Napoleonic Wars when the British Fleet blockaded the French ports and cut off the supply of coffee.

CORN SALAD / LAMB'S LETTUCE / MÂCHE
Valerianella locusta (Valerianaceae)

Wild corn salad is an annual which grows throughout Europe and Western Asia; in parts of Northern Europe it is a common weed, freely growing in fields and roadsides. It has a long history as a salad plant, particularly in France where it has several common names and there are traditional corn salad recipes.

It germinates and grows best in cool conditions and is very hardy, excellent for cut–and–come–again winter and spring use if sown in late summer. Its small flowers are misty blue and cultivated varieties usually have larger leaves than the wild forms – those with darker green stiffer leaves are said to be the hardiest. Italian Corn Salad is probably a distinct species.

Verte de Cambral

A traditional French variety that forms tight rosettes of bright green leaves. A decorative and unusual salad plant, whole rosettes should be harvested when they have 6–8 leaves.

Coquille de Louviers

This corn salad has very dark green spoon-shaped leaves. It is extremely hardy, and can be harvested all through the winter.

Grote Noordhollande

This popular corn salad forms spreading rosettes with very dark green outer leaves and paler centres.

Italian Corn Salad

A very distinctive traditional variety with blond leaves and a pronounced flavour. It is very productive. but less hardy than green-leaved varieties. Ideal for milder climates, this variety will grow successfully from the Atlantic coast of Europe up to Belgium.

OTHER SALADS

Venus' Looking Glass *Legousia speculum-veneris*
Also known as **Rapunzel,** this little-known plant is used like corn salad, and can be harvested early in the year. It used to be widely grown as a vegetable and can still occasionally be found growing wild in grain fields, but it is now in danger of extinction.

Rucola Selvatica *Diplotaxis spp*
Another useful addition to salads, traditionally served in Europe with goat's cheese. It can also be used as a leaf vegetable.

CUCUMBERS & GHERKINS
Cucumis sativus (Cucurbitaceae)

Cucumbers originate from India, where many wild forms still grow. There are records of their cultivation in China and the Middle East around 4000 years ago, and they were popular with the Ancient Greeks and Romans. Fruits vary in colour and shape, and can be white, yellow or green, long or oval. The early varieties frequently had rough skins and spines.

In 19th century England, cucumbers were extensively cultivated in hot beds under glass and long smooth glasshouse or 'frame' cucumbers were developed. Their male flowers had to be removed as fruits were very bitter fruit if pollination occurred. These have largely been superseded by modern all-female hybrid glasshouse cucumbers. Outdoor or 'ridge' cucumbers are generally hardier and much easier to grow. Gherkins are a type of ridge cucumber with prickly skins, and their flesh tends to be drier; they are picked small for pickling.

All cucumbers need fertile soil with good drainage and plenty of moisture, especially when they are fruiting. They are frost tender and the seeds generally need high temperatures, over 20°C (68°F) to germinate. In cool areas, sow them in pots indoors and transplant them to a sunny sheltered spot outdoors, or to a glasshouse or polytunnel. They can be trained up trellis or netting, or left to trail over the ground. Cucumbers will cross-pollinate with other cucumber varieties over long distances, but individual blooms can be hand-pollinated and isolated for saving seed in the same way as squashes (*see Chapter 5, pages 90–97*).

OUTDOOR VARIETIES

Boothby's Blonde

This distinctive cucumber was grown for several generations by the Boothby family in Maine, US, but it only became commercially available in the mid 1990s, after it was taken up by a couple of small US seed companies with an interest in old varieties. The fruits are 14–20cm (6–8in) long, oval with blunt ends, and flesh is and flesh is sweet and delicious. Skin is creamy yellow coloured and warty with small black spines. This variety will produce without continuous sunshine, it is early and productive, and ideal for northern climates.

Lemon / Lemon Apple

Originally from Australia, these small lemon-shaped fruit have pale yellow skins and very crisp white flesh. They have a mild crunchy texture and thin skin so you can eat them like an apple, or use them in salads or for pickling. Very productive plants are more tolerant of drought than most varieties. Although traditionally an outdoor variety, these may be best grown under glass.

Crystal Apple

Similar to **Lemon**, and sometimes confused with it, this heavy cropping variety originally came from New Zealand. Round, prickly-skinned fruits are creamy-white with tender green-white flesh and very mild flavour. Like **Lemon**, this variety is very adaptable to most climates, including short-season areas and where water is limited.

GLASSHOUSE / FRAME VARIETIES

Butcher's Disease Resisting

This variety was developed in Southern England in 1903, as a way of combatting leaf spot disease, to which it is resistant. It is a delicious and productive cucumber in its own right, and ideal if there is any risk of infection in your glasshouse.

Telegraph/Improved Telegraph

In 1868 this was recommended as the very best variety for cooler climates, producing fruits late into the autumn. Mid-green fruits are very straight, crisp and well-flavoured.

Conqueror

First marketed in 1872, crispy green fruits grow reliably in lower temperatures than other frame varieties. This is a very good traditional variety with excellent flavour.

PICKLING CUCUMBERS / GHERKINS

Early Russian

Coming to Europe from America, where it arrived from Russia in the 1850s, this variety is probably the best for short-season areas. One of the earliest pickling cucumbers on record, it is primarily used for dill pickle but can be used for slicing. Fruits are slender and short ovals, up to 12cm (5in) long, with mid-green skin. Train the vigorous plants on a trellis to produce all season if you keep picking them – the flesh does not get bitter as the season progresses.

Delikatess

This medium-sized variety originally came from Holland. Although it can be used for slicing, it is best used for pickling. Fruits have smooth shiny skin and very good flavour.

Cornichon de Bourbonne

This old variety has been traditionally used throughout France as the most popular pickling cucumber for well over a century. Primarily used to make gourmet sour cornichon pickles, the fruits should be picked as soon as they are 5–7cm (2–3in) long.

Langelands Kaempe Giant

A traditional Danish variety, long narrow dark green gherkins with smooth skins are produced in great numbers on outdoor plants.

ENDIVE
Cichorium endivia (Compositae)

Endive is closely related to chicory. There is some confusion over its origin, but it was probably first domesticated in Central Asia and has a long history of cultivation in Southern Europe. Endives are annual or biennial plants, producing attractive rosettes of leaves which are usually used in salads.

There are two main types of endive: curly-leaved or frisée endive, and broad-leaved Batavian endive or Escarole. The curled types are less hardy and are best used for summer harvests in cool climates. Broad-leaved endives will stand more frost and are a valuable autumn and winter crop.

Endives are traditionally blanched by tying up the leaves or covering them to exclude light. This makes the leaves sweeter, but is not always necessary, depending on taste; the central leaves of many varieties are naturally part blanched.

They are self-pollinating, although endives will cross-pollinate with other endives, but not with chicory.

BROAD-LEAVED BATAVIAN ENDIVE

Cornet de Bordeaux
A very hardy fine old French variety. It is ideal as a cut-and-come-again salad green throughout the winter, or it will form a small head. It is particularly useful if grown in a cold tunnel or cloche.

Cornet d'Anjou
An old French variety which is similar in taste and appearance to **Cornet de Bordeaux** although it has slightly larger leaves and grows a taller head. It is marginally less hardy.

Géante Maraichère Bossa
Attractive light green plants have a bright yellow heart, and can be used all year round. Sow under glass for winter and spring harvest, outside for summer and autumn use.

CURLY-LEAVED ENDIVE / FRISÉE

Frisée de Ruffec / Green Curled Ruffec
Mentioned in the 1860s, deeply cut dark green leaves with white midribs grow in a thick rosette. It tolerates cold wet weather, and will stand through a mild winter if protected with a light mulch or a cloche. It is a good variety for autumn harvest.

Très Fine Maraichère
This small compact variety is very frizzy and decorative, with a pleasant, slightly sharp, flavour. Grow it like lettuce and other summer salads as it is not hardy.

Frisée d'Eté à Coeur Jaune
A vigorous old variety with a very attractive pale yellow heart. It is good for blanching, very resistant to pests, and will grow reliably for summer and autumn harvest in cool areas and at high altitudes.

FENNEL
Foeniculum vulgare var *dulce (Umbelliferae)*

As the name suggests, the varieties of Florence fennel grown today originate in Italy, where the vegetable has been in cultivation for many centuries. It is an annual, grown mainly for its swollen leaf bases which form a bulb just above ground level. This is used both as a cooked vegetable and in salads. The plant also has attractive feathery foliage which can be cut for flavouring.

Florence fennel is not easy to grow well. It does best on rich, well drained soil and needs plenty of moisture throughout its growth. Most traditional varieties are sensitive to daylength and will bolt before forming a bulb if sown before mid-summer. Lack of water and fluctuating temperatures can also cause premature bolting. Plants will withstand light frost, and a second sowing for autumn harvest can be made in mild areas.

Précoce d'Eté
No longer on the European List, this fennel is the best for coldest climates. Sow it when the soil is really warm, through May and June, for harvest as soon as it forms a bulb. It tastes very sweet, with a lingering flavour of aniseed or licorice.

Perfection / Mammoth Perfection
This Florence Fennel produces very large white bulbs with a delicate flavour. It is easy to grow, performs well on most soils, and it is very slow to bolt.

Sirio / Romy
There is some confusion about the names of many old Italian varieties, which may also be known simply as **Florence Fennel**. Look out for this sweet and aromatic variety which produces very large solid round bulbs on compact plants. It is fast growing and matures early.

Di Firenze
Another old Italian variety with slightly smaller bulbs than **Sirio**, otherwise very similar.

GARLIC

Allium sativum var *sativum* & *Allium sativum* var *ophioscordon* (Alliaceae)

Believed to have originated from an Allium found growing wild in Central Asia, garlic has been cultivated for millennia in East and West. It was depicted on the pyramids in Ancient Egypt, where it was part of the rations provided for the labourers building the pyramids, and the Chinese are known to have grown it since at least 3000BC. In some areas of Europe it is part of traditional folklore, seen as a talisman against witchcraft.

In Europe most garlics are soft-necked garlics, which do not form a flower stalk and have a soft braidable neck. They are very productive, usually producing bulbs made up of numerous smaller cloves in overlapping layers, which store well. Hardneck garlics are those which produce a flower stalk, and although they rarely set seed, they often form a cluster of bulblets in the flowerhead. Picking off these flower stalks will encourage the growth of the underground bulb, which is usually formed of a few large cloves. The stalks are edible, and in China they are a valued crop. Rocambole is an unusual form of hardneck garlic with a very coiled stem. Its bulb and bulblets can be used like garlic and its chive-like leaves for garnishing..

Most garlic is propagated by planting individual cloves in autumn or early spring as a cold period is generally needed before good bulbs will form – the plants are remarkably hardy, surviving temperatures of -10°C (14°F). In France, garlic is traditionally planted on 10th November and harvested on 20th June. It needs a rich, light, well drained soil, but do not plant garlic in soil that has been freshly manured.

There are many local strains of garlic, white-skinned or pink-tinged. Garlic will adapt to the daylength and to the temperature over a number of years, so it can be worth developing your own strain by saving and planting cloves from the healthiest plants.

Germidour

An old French variety for autumn planting. It produces large purple bulbs each with 10–15 cloves. It stores well for at least 6 months without deterioration.

Thermidrome

One of the traditional varieties from Southeastern France, it produces large white bulbs, each with around 10 cloves.

Printanor

This pink-cloved variety from the Auvergne is resistant to pests and diseases, has excellent flavour and stores particularly well if dried thoroughly in the sun or in an airy shed.

Rose de Lautrec

This hardneck garlic produces a flower stem as well as attractive pink-skinned bulbs which store well.

HAMBURG PARSLEY
Petroselinum crispum tuberosum (Umbelliferae)

A type of parsley grown for its thick fleshy roots, resembling those of a small parsnip. A relatively recent vegetable, it has traditionally been popular in Germany and Eastern Europe since the late 19th century. Roots are good in soups and stews, and parsley-like leaves can be used like herb parsley. Hamburg parsley has never been an important commercial crop, so no traditional varieties are listed.

Hamburg parsley grows best on light, well-cultivated soil. Seeds are sown in mid to late spring and the roots are normally ready for lifting in the autumn. They are hardy, and can normally be left in the ground until required unless winters are severe. The plants are biennial, producing umbels of small flowers the summer after sowing.

KALE
Brassica oleracea var *acephela (Cruciferae)*

Kale is derived from the cabbage which grows wild on the coasts of the Mediterranean and Adriatic Seas, and may have been the first cultivated brassica. It was widely grown by the Greeks and Romans and has long been valued in Northern Europe for its hardiness. Kale leaves can be picked throughout the winter and many types also produce delicate young shoots in spring, providing a useful green vegetable when little else is available.

Kale thrives in rich well drained soil, although it will tolerate poorer conditions than most brassicas. Seed is usually sown in a seedbed in late spring to early summer and the seedlings transplanted to their permanent positions in mid to late summer. The recent fashion for ornamental kales in various combinations is not new; in *The Vegetable Garden* (1885), Vilmorin describes red and white variegated 'garnishing' kales.

Most kales are biennial, but a few will last for several seasons in the right conditions. Like other related brassicas they are not easy to save for seed or keep true to type (*see Chapter 5, pages 90-97*).

Ragged Jack

This ancient variety has been known in Europe for centuries. Plants have deeply ruffled grey-green leaves with purple veins. In the coldest weather the leaves all turn reddish-purple. The leaves are exceptionally tender, but should be used straight after picking. In milder climates **Ragged Jack** will grow all year round.

Asparagus Kale

Listed in Vilmorin's *The Vegetable Garden* in 1885, this is still reputed to be one of the tastiest and most tender kales. The leaves can be eaten over the winter, but it is best left until spring when you can harvest the tender shoots out of the leaf axils, and eat them like asparagus. As well as spring sowing, you can direct-seed this variety in July or August for a late crop.

Cottager's Kale

Recently dropped from the English National List, this unusual variety was originally bred in the 1850s in Oxfordshire by crossing Brussels sprouts with a kale variety. Plants stand 1.25m (4ft) tall, and produce a profusion of blue-green rosette-like shoots.

Nero di Toscana / Palm Tree Cabbage

Highly ornamental, plants can grow to 2m (6$\frac{1}{2}$ft) tall, topped by a bouquet of thin dark green leaves about 60cm (2ft) long. These all grow from the same point at the top of the stalk, so that plants look like miniature palm trees. Although it is often grown as an annual, this variety can continue growing for 2–3 years.

Thousand Headed

A strong-growing, hardy and prolific variety, which originated in Northern France, where it was traditionally used for stock feeding as well as for table use. Plants grow 1–1.25m (3–4ft) tall, and branches along the stems produce numerous large, smooth, dark green tender leaves.

Schwarzkohl

A hardy variety from Germany, a very popular green vegetable before imported greens were plentiful. It is very decorative, with large deep green ruffled leaves, so could provide attractive colour through winter in the ornamental garden as well as guaranteeing good yields for months.

Westfalian

Another hardy heritage kale from Germany, this huge variety provides masses of fresh greens throughout the winter. The young leaves and side shoots are the best for eating, largest leaves tend to be slightly tough.

Altmärker *(Brassica oleracea* var *sabellica)*

Varieties with red or reddish foliage are rare in Central Europe. This German variety is very tall and the stalks are used as walking sticks. The foliage is not strongly curled and is used as a vegetable. An Eastern European variety, **Krasnaya Kuroavafa Vysokaja**, is tall with red, curled leaves.

KOHL RABI

Brassica oleracea var *gongylodes (Cruciferae)*

Kohl rabi is another cabbage-related vegetable, but it is selected for its swollen stem base; this makes it look more like a turnip than a cabbage, although it is much sweeter. It was first recorded in Europe in the 16th century, but was never very popular in England or France – 19th century cookery books treated it as a novelty rather in the same way as books do today; it has always been more widely grown in Germany and Eastern Europe.

The 'root' can be eaten as a hot vegetable, or raw in salads, and the young leaves can be used as greens. Kohl rabi prefers light fertile soils, with plenty of moisture. It is quick growing and several sowings can be made from early spring to mid summer, to get a continuous supply. Purple-skinned types tend to be the hardiest, tolerating moderate frosts. Most varieties are best harvested young, before they reach tennis ball size.

White Vienna / Green Vienna
Slightly earlier than the purple strain, the creamy-white flesh is very sweet and mild. Best harvested young, this versatile vegetable is good in stews and soups, or grated in salads.

Purple Vienna
This variety has a purple skin and white flesh. Sow seed from early to late summer as it is reasonably frost resistant and can be harvested through early winter.

Gigante / Gigante Winter
This huge Czechoslovakian heritage variety usually grows larger than 4.5kg (10lb), and can get to around 27kg (60lb)! Despite its vast size, the crisp white flesh remains tender and mild-flavoured, with no tough or woody fibre. Abundant greens can be used like kale or winter greens.

LEEKS
Allium porrum (Alliaceae)

Leeks probably originated in the near East, where they have been cultivated since ancient times, and they have been grown in Europe for many centuries. It was the victory of King Cadwallader over the Saxons in 640AD which led to the Welsh association with the vegetable – apparently during this battle Welshmen wore leeks in their hats to distinguish their men from the enemy.

Leeks are a very hardy winter vegetable, thriving in fertile soils containing plenty of organic matter. Large leeks require a long growing season, so seed is generally sown in a seedbed from early to late spring for planting out in early to mid summer in individual holes, but leeks for harvesting young and small can be direct-sown. They can be harvested from early autumn to late spring, unless winters are exceptionally severe. Although there are some exceptions, early varieties usually have longer white shafts and paler foliage, and to be less hardy. Traditional varieties of late leeks often have deep green or blue-green leaves, although Bleu de Solaise, (*see right*) is an early and less hardy variety.

Leeks are biennial, producing magnificent round seedheads the summer after sowing. The flowers will cross-pollinate with other leeks, but not with onions, so it is not difficult to save their seed.

Bleu de Solaise

The blue-green leaves of this attractive old French variety turn violet-purple in cold weather. Particularly good for short-season areas, this early maturing variety is excellent for late autumn and early winter harvest, but it will also withstand some frost.

Gros Jaune de Poitou

An old variety originating in the west of France, grown extensively at the end of the last century. It is quick growing, developing a short thick stem with distinctive yellowy green foliage. This is best for autumn cropping, as it is not very hardy.

The Lyon / Prizetaker

An old English favourite, this was introduced in 1886. It has very tall foliage, and long thick tender white stems, which retain a good mild flavour. Grow it for autumn use.

Monstreux de Carentan / Giant Carentan

An excellent old French variety, which produces extremely tender thick white stems about 20cm (8in) tall. Reliable even in freezing conditions, it is very productive and hardy.

Musselburgh

In demand since the 1820s, this is a very reliable and versatile variety, producing good thick stems with marked flavour, in most climates and conditions.

Babbington Leek

This is not a true leek, but possibly the wild form of **Elephant Garlic**. Green shoots can be cut and eaten like leeks; bulbs can be lifted and stored to be used as a type of mild garlic. Bulbils are produced prolifically below ground and in the flower head, the latter being easiest to propagate from as those from the base tend to remain dormant for a year or so. Plant bulbils during the winter where they are to grow, leaving them plenty of room as they are a perennial crop and can be left in the ground for many years. When well established, a huge flower spike of up to 2m (6ft) is produced, above which attractive purple flowers bloom, followed by pale green bulbils.

Perennial French Leek *Allium ampeloprasum*

Similar to the **Babbington Leek,** this member of the onion family is also grown for the garlic like cloves which form at the base of the flower stalk. They have an unusual consistency, somewhere between garlic and turnip. The larger cloves are used for soups and vegetable stews, the smaller ones are replanted. It is quite common in France and near the French–German border. When the flower stalk appears, it has to be cut back to allow the cloves to develop properly. Cloves are planted in late summer and will overwinter.

LETTUCES
Lactuca sativa

Our present day lettuces are probably derived from the wild lettuce *Lactuca serriola*, although their origin is uncertain – the Mediterranean, the near East and Siberia have all been suggested as homelands. Portrayed on stone carvings in Ancient Egypt, lettuces were also valued by Greeks and Romans, for medicinal and culinary uses. The Romans reputedly introduced the cos or romaine lettuce, with its head of erect leaves, so-called because it originated on the Greek island of Cos (Kos).

Butterhead lettuces have soft leaves and flat rounded heads, crisphead varieties have round heads with crisp wrinkled leaves; however, some traditional varieties fall between these categories. Non-heading or loose-leaved lettuces are also popular today, but they are not new – at least five varieties were known in Northern Europe 100 years ago. Less familiar is the stem lettuce, which comes from China; this is not grown for its leaves but for its thick central stem which can be sliced and cooked, or may be used raw in salads in the same way as radishes or cucumbers.

Lettuces like fertile moisture-retentive soil, and prefer light shade in hot summers as they are a cool weather crop. Non-hearting types are generally most tolerant of heat and poor soils. Few lettuce varieties withstand more than a very light frost, although some of the old winter types are relatively hardy. To maintain a regular supply of lettuce, you should sow seed at intervals from early spring to late summer, germinating the seed indoors if temperatures are too low (in spring) or too hot (in midsummer).

Annual and self-pollinating, lettuce is very easy to save for seed, and cross-pollination is rarely a problem as long as different varieties are separated by 2–3m (6–10ft).

COS LETTUCES

Stoke

This small lettuce is extremely hardy and capable of overwintering through to the North of France, Belgium and the Netherlands, and the South of England. It was grown for over 150 years by the Cheeseman family in Stoke, near Rochester, in England, but probably dates back long before they started to grow it. It has a good texture and flavour.

Bath Cos

Originating before 1880, this is a deliciously meaty and crunchy cos lettuce which can grow very large in the summer. The flavour of the largest specimens can be improved by tying up the head to blanch the inner leaves. It was praised in *The Gardener* magazine in 1867 as the "sort that should be in every garden. No other variety can surpass it or approach it for general use… Thrown into a heap on snowy linen, it looks a rich crystalline, frothy pile, and cannot fail to be a tempting and refreshing bite for the hungry sportsman after a hard day's labour".

Ballon / Balloon

A very large French variety with a huge heart. Despite its size, this is very tender and delicious. Good for hotter climates, this variety rarely runs to seed.

Matchless / Bunyards Matchless

The leaves of this unusual-looking variety have a kink in them so they curve round to form an open heart rather than the usual upright cos-type leaves. This lettuce stands well without bolting or losing flavour, and can be grown all the year round, particularly good for autumn or spring sowing.

Lobjoits Green Cos / Romaine Gris Maraichère

Praised by Vilmorin in *The Vegetable Garden* in 1885, the leaves of this lettuce are tall, crisp, sweet and very dark green.

OTHER HEADING LETTUCES

Brune d'Hiver

This French lettuce, a traditional favourite since the 1850s, is midway between a butterhead and cos type. It has excellent flavour and colour, with green leaves bronzed at the tips. One of the hardiest of all, it is ideal for cold season areas, but may bolt in hotter climates.

Merveille de Quatre Saisons

An unusual old French lettuce, the outer leaves are reddish-green with cranberry red tips, and tight hearts are creamy-coloured. The heads form quickly and stay in good condition for a long time in cool weather. This variety does tend to bolt in hot weather, but still holds its good flavour. It is ideal for summer sowings.

Tom Thumb

Small plants produce compact, crisp, tightly furled heads about the size of a tennis ball. This dwarf black-seeded variety was named after a famous American midget from Barnum's circus in the 1850s, although some American sources say that it is an English heirloom! It is an extremely attractive garnishing lettuce with sweet, bright green crumpled leaves. Or one lettuce is the perfect size for a single serving of salad. It is best for spring sowings.

Grosse Blonde Parasseuse

Old round-headed variety with very pale green-white leaves, and almost white outer leaves. It grows very large, typically attaining a diameter of 30cm (12in), and grows very well in hot sun without bolting.

Chou de Naples / Sant Angelo

This old variety is the parent of most 'modern' crisphead lettuces, including **Iceberg**, and the English favourite, Webb's Wonder, introduced in 1890. The head is slightly squashed with very pale leaves, while the outer ones are very ruffled on the edges. A late variety, it is very slow to bolt – if you want to collect the white seeds you need to force it by stripping off the outer leaves.

Iceberg / Batavia Blonde

This original crisp headed lettuce, known since the 1850s, bears little resemblance to the variety known as Iceberg popularly sold in supermarkets. This is a tasty garden variety with compact light green heads made up of crisp leaves with a slight bronze fringe. This good reliable variety is essentially a summer lettuce, as it is tolerant of heat. It is also has a good resistance to many pests and diseases, including downy mildew.

Loos Tennis Ball / Gotte de Loos à graine blanche / White Seeded Tennis Ball / Boston Market Lettuce

Loos Tennis Ball and a number of other lettuces may be synonyms, as **Tennis Balls** form an old category of lettuce types, rather than referring to a specific variety. This is a classic, cabbage-headed lettuce with a long history, apparently grown in the 1790s in Thomas Jefferson's garden at Monticello in the US and apparently very popular in France and Belgium in the 19th century. **Loos Tennis Ball** is moderately tender with medium green smooth leaves forming a loose head with a solid centre. It is resistant to mildew so can be grown well in glasshouses and frames.

Craquerelle du Midi

A crisp and crunchy open-hearted old French lettuce with deep green crisp and crunchy leaves. Particularly suited to continental climates, it will also resist some frost. A superb garden variety, it can be sown from January through to August.

All Year Round

This is a hardy variety, perfect for late autumn and early spring harvesting. Medium-sized with a solid head and pale green foliage, it is a very old and reliable variety for all cooler climates. It originated in France, and in the 1880s was one of the most commonly grown there.

LOOSE-LEAF LETTUCES

Bronze Arrow / Bronze Arrowhead

A very old variety from the West coast of the US. Tender, sweet and delicious, the large dark green leaves are blotched in bronze, and pointed like an arrowhead. It is hardy and adaptable to most climates, and stands well without bolting in hot weather.

Feuille de Chêne / Oak Leaf

Pre-1900 variety, an old favourite with good reason: thick rosettes of deeply lobed medium-green leaves stay sweet and tender with no bitterness. Its willingness to withstand heat means you can reap a long harvest throughout the summer.

Red Deer Tongue

Once a common garden variety, this is now regaining popularity: slightly-savoyed sweet and tender tri-angular red leaves grow in a rosette around a loose cream coloured head. **Deer Tongue** is very attractive and a reliable producer, tolerant of heat and cold.

Langue de Canari

This very unusual variety is worth growing for its attractive pale green leaves which are serrated like those of a dandelion. Flavour is good, and it is resistant to mildew.

Gebl Salat

This distinctively flavoured open-headed lettuce is grown widely in Croatia and Slovenia, and in the south of Austria. It is light green, with attractive pointed and jagged leaves. It is slow to bolt and withstands heat well. Despite its qualities, consumer preference for heading varieties in the areas where **Gebl Salat** is traditionally grown, mean that this good variety is becoming endangered.

Forellen Schluss

This fine-flavoured attractive lettuce has light green leaves speckled with maroon. It is an old heritage variety from Austria.

MELONS
Cucumis melo (Cucurbitaceae)

Melons probably originated in tropical Africa, but were introduced at least 2000 years ago to Central Asia, where many cultivated forms developed. Despite the fact that they need cossetting in cool climates, melons have been grown in Northern Europe since the Middle Ages, and dozens of different varieties were known in 19th century France and in Britain, where the heated glasshouses of Victorian kitchen gardens produced some excellently flavoured fruit.

In most of Northern Europe melons need to be grown under cover; canteloupe varieties are more cold tolerant than others. Seeds need temperatures of around 21°C (70°F) in order to germinate, and seedlings must be grown on at temperatures above 13°C (55°F). Plants can be grown along the ground or trained up trellising or netting. They need a fertile well drained soil, and plenty of moisture while the fruits are swelling, although you should reduce watering when the fruit start to ripen.

Like squashes, melons have separate male and female flowers on each plant and they easily cross–pollinate with other melons. Hand-pollination is less easy than for squashes (*see page 94*).

Blenheim Orange

First introduced to Blenheim Palace in Oxfordshire, England, in 1881 by the Duke of Marlborough's gardener, this melon was a traditional glasshouse favourite for half a century in England. Medium-sized red fleshed fruits grow steadily even in cool weather, and this variety is highly productive. Thick, very succulent flesh is sweet and highly perfumed, with a delicate fine-grained texture.

Hero of Lockinge

Suitable for a heated or cool glasshouse, this 19th century English melon was only dropped from the National List in 1995. It is a richly flavoured white fleshed melon, an heirloom which reminds us of English Victorian kitchen gardens. It was probably developed by the head gardener of the Lockinge Estate in Oxfordshire, England.

Noir des Carmes / Early Black Rock

A 19th century French early-fruiting variety, also suitable for a heated or cool glasshouse. Fruits are almost spherical, slightly flattened at the ends with a smooth very dark green skin. Flesh is orange, thick, sweet and highly perfumed.

De Bellegarde

A very old early-fruiting variety with medium-sized oblong fruits, orange splashed with green before they ripen. Reasonably tolerant of cool weather, the flesh is reddish-orange and very sweet.

Extra Early Nutmeg

This very old outdoor variety is in danger of extinction. Yet the flavour of the sweet greenish-orange flesh is excellent, and it is very early – maturing in 61–63 days from planting. It is worth seeking this one out.

Streits Freilandmelone Grüngenetzt

This Austrian variety was developed by the breeder and seedsman Streit earlier this century. Melons are small and covered with a green net, and have been selected for growing outdoors or in a cold frame. Although they will ripen satisfactorily in Northern Europe, the sugar content is higher where it is warmer.

Ananas d'Amerique à Chair Rouge

These tiny melons reach no more than 10cm (4in) diameter. The skin is mottled green and cream, with distinctive ribs, and the flesh is incredibly sweet, perfumed and juicy. Grow in a heated glasshouse in northern climates to produce an abundant crop.

Jenny Lind

Dating back to the 1840s, this is a very popular American heirloom. Flattened turban shaped 0.5–1.5kg (1–3lb) muskmelon fruits are produced prolifically on 1.75m (5ft) vines. Green-fleshed and very sweet, fruits mature midseason, but although this is traditionally grown as an outdoor variety, in cooler areas the vines are unreliable so for best results it is advisable to grow **Jenny Lind** under glass.

Sucrin de Tours

A reasonably early variety, spherical fruits are covered with distinctive fine netting. Sweet flesh is red with a firm texture. These can be grown in a heated or cool glasshouse, or outdoors in warmer areas.

Large White Prescott

This French canteloupe used to be a favourite for market gardeners, but is sadly now rare. Large lumpy melons have pale green-white skin, ribbed and warted, with sweet fragrant orange flesh. It would be good to see these coming back into circulation, as they are exceptional quality, and will grow outdoors, ripening even in periods of fairly cool weather.

OCA
Oxalis tuberosa (Oxalidaceae)

Oca is native to the Andes in South America. It has small wrinkled tubers with white, red or yellow skin, which can be baked or boiled, and some varieties can be eaten raw. Oca have an acid taste and in their homeland they are typically dried for a few days in the sun to sweeten them.

Although oca were known in Europe in the last century, they have never been widely grown. Tubers are planted in spring; the foliage is frost tender, so they can be started off in pots indoors in areas with a short growing season.

The plants are sometimes earthed up during growth, like potatoes. In Northern Europe tubers do not start to swell until late in the season (possibly because of the effect of daylength) and have to be lifted after the first frosts in autumn, so yields can be low .

Named varieties are not listed, but strains with different skin colours can be found, and it may be worth saving tubers and trying to develop your own, adapted to local conditions.

OKRA
Hibiscus esculentus (Malvaceae)

Okra is native to tropical Africa, where it has been used for thousands of years. It crossed to America with the slave trade and from there to Southern Europe. The American name 'gumbo', used for both the okra pods and the stew-like dishes containing them, comes from an African word 'ngombo'.

Okra need fertile soil and warm humid conditions to thrive. In Northern Europe they can be grown with protection, but few varieties are available. One compensation for probably poor yields from okra plants is their eye-catching yellow flowers. The pods which follow must be picked for eating when young, otherwise they become fibrous.

Clemson's Spineless

Probably the most popular variety of okra, producing a heavy crop of high quality, dark green, lightly grooved spineless pods. Pick pods when they are only 6–9cm (2–3in) long, or they will be tough.

Burgundy

Highly attractive and productive plants can reach 1.2m (7ft) tall, with green leaves striped in red. Fruits grow to about 10cm (4in), and are exceptionally tender.

COMMON / BULB ONIONS & MULTIPLIER ONIONS
Allium cepa & Allium fistulosum (Alliaceae)

The origins of our familiar bulb onion *Allium cepa* is uncertain, but it is thought that they were first cultivated in Asia, probably Iran and Southern Russia. Certainly they were grown in Ancient Egypt about 3000BC, and by the Greeks and Romans. Their health-giving properties have been recognised as long as their edible qualities – the earliest herbalists recommended onions for their cleansing effect on the body.

To produce large bulbs, onions need fertile, well-drained soil and a long growing season. Seed is usually sown in early spring, indoors with heat in cool climates. Plant seedlings out in mid to late spring. The growth of bulb onions depends on daylength, which makes regionally adapted varieties important. In traditional European varieties, the leaf growth stops at the end of June, once the days start to shorten, and thereafter the bulbs start to swell. The bulbs can be pulled for use at any stage, but they are ready to harvest for storage in late summer, once the foliage begins to die back and the tops bend over. As long as they are dried thoroughly, onion bulbs should last in storage for seven or eight months.

Some old onion varieties were traditionally sown in August to overwinter and give an early summer crop the following year, but these have largely been replaced by hardier, early maturing modern varieties. All bulb onions are biennial, producing handsome globe-shaped flowerheads in their second season. The flowers are pollinated by insects and will cross-pollinate with other onion varieties.

Other types of onion include those variously called multiplier onions, shallots and potato onions (*Allium cepa* var *Aggregatum*) where the bulbs divide and multiply laterally. There are many similar but distinct forms, and the classifications are not clear. All are relatively trouble-free to grow and easy to propagate; simply replant the small bulbs in spring.

Egyptian onions, or tree onions (*Allium cepa* var *proliferum*) produce clusters of small aerial bulbs instead of flowers, and these can be used for eating or propagation. These bulbs are tiny compared to those of common onions, but the plants are extremely hardy, and bulbs and foliage can be picked throughout most winters.

Welsh onions, ciboule or Japanese bunching onions (*Allium fistulosum*) are grown for their leaves and stems. They were cultivated in China more than 2000 years ago before being introduced to Japan, then probably into Europe during the Middle Ages. *A. fistulosum* are perennials, and can be propagated by seed or by dividing the clumps. They tend to be reasonably tolerant of cool as well as extremely hot temperatures, and these are still the principal types of onions grown in China and Japan.

COMMON / BULB ONIONS

Giant Zittau

Dating back to the 1870s, this is one of the best of all keeping onions. Attractive golden-skinned bulbs are almost round in this white Spanish-type onion, and flavour is very good, even after long storage.

Rousham Park Hero

This fine old onion is pale yellow-skinned, often described as 'straw-coloured', and shaped like a flattened globe. It grows to a good size, up to 1.25kg (2.5lb), with excellent flavour. Popular with gardeners throughout England towards the end of the 19th century, it was the top exhibition onion for many years. Rousham Park Hero is very hardy, good for spring or autumn sowings, and keeps well.

Up-to-Date

A long-established variety, renowned for its taste and keeping qualities. It is globe shaped with pale brown skin, and its flavour is strong and distinctive – Lawrence Hill, the founder of the Henry Doubleday Research Association said that it was so strong that "one good breath of them could slam the garden gate"! It has some resistance to white rot.

James Longkeeping

First listed in 1793, this English variety was originally selected to last well through long winters. It will keep its condition well in storage, without noticeable deterioration in appearance or flavour, for up to nine months. The skin of this strongly flavoured variety is reddish-brown.

Southport Red Globe

Introduced to Europe from America, probably in the 1880s, this blood red onion grows to a large size, and has traditionally been popular with gardeners wishing to exhibit at vegetable shows. It is a good keeper.

Jaune Paille des Vertus

This was one of the varieties which were grown in great quantities to be sold at the Parisian markets in the late 19th century, and it still retains its popularity today. Medium-sized globes are yellow-brown skinned, of uniform size, dense, well flavoured, and store well. This is a very reliable variety for spring sowing.

Paris Silverskin

This perfectly round miniature onion is skinless and thin-necked – a gourmet onion, very early and delicious. Use fresh and for pickling. These are very easy to grow and do not need thinning.

Red and Yellow Laaer Zwiebel

The **Laaer** onion is an Austrian speciality; it has disease resistances which have been used in many European breeding programmes. Grown on the sandy soils of Eastern Austria, it has excellent storage qualities.

SHALLOTS

Allium cepa var aggregatum

Hâtive de Niort

This is the classic exhibition shallot. Long flask-shaped bulbs are a regular and uniform size with deep brown skins. The flavour is very good, and this variety appears resistant to rot.

Cuisse de Poulet

This old French variety has large elongated bulbs – presumably said to resemble a chicken's thigh! The flavour of this snow-white fleshed variety is good, and these small onions store well.

Jersey Onion shallot

Traditionally considered the best shallot for pickling and cooking, this Channel Island variety has white flesh blotched with pinkish red, and a distinctive strong flavour. These shallots store well.

Pearl Onions *Allium porrum* var *sectivum*

Pearl onions are small rounded white onions which used to be widely grown for pickling, but have now almost vanished from our gardens. They do not set seeds and should be dug up in mid to late summer and replanted closely together to produce a crop the following year. They are particularly suitable for small vegetable gardens.

OTHER ONIONS

Eschlauch *Allium ascalonicum*

This perennial onion is frequently confused with the shallot or potato onion. It is an endangered species, grows in vineyards in Eastern Europe and is used like chives. There are no known varieties.

ORACHE
Atriplex hortensis (Chenopodiaceae)

This ancient vegetable originates in Asia and temperate Europe, and probably reached Northern Europe in the Middle Ages, when the young leaves were often used as a 'pot herb' (leafy vegetable). It is a quick-growing annual with large triangular leaves of red or green. You can use the leaves in salads or as a substitute for spinach. Plants are wind-pollinated and selfseed prolifically.

Red Orache

This is a very decorative annual plant, up to 2m (6ft) tall, with very deep red pointed leaves and tiny reddish flowers. Eat the young leaves raw in salads or cook them like spinach.

Belle Dame / Arroche Blonde

This is a very old pale green leaved variety with white flowers, otherwise similar to the red variety above.

ORIENTAL GREENS
Brassica rapa / Brassica juncea (Cruciferae)

Oriental greens developed over a long period of cultivation in China and Japan, and form an amazingly diverse group of vegetables. Although some had reached Europe by the 19th century, they were not widely grown, despite the fact they are fast growing and reasonably hardy. They are well suited to cropping in autumn and spring in cool climates, when fresh leafy vegetables are limited, and are invaluable in salads and stir-fries.

Chinese cabbage and pak choi are the most familiar types in the West, only recently introduced although they have been growing in China for at least 2000 years. The original varieties would have been loose-headed ragged types, the large tight-headed varieties commonly sold in Europe today came much later, and the majority are F1 hybrids. Pak choi is reputedly even older than Chinese cabbage, and only a small selection of the varieties available in China can be found in the West.

Mustard greens are thought to have come from the Himalayas. Many types were developed over the years, some for their seed pods and others for their peppery leaves, and they are highly valued in Chinese cooking. The milder mizuna and mibuna probably originated in China, but have a long history of cultivation in Japan and are often referred to as 'Japanese greens'.

Tatsoi / Rosette Pak Choi

A distinctive plant, believed to be of ancient origin. It forms a compact thick rosette of small dark spoon-shaped leaves. Reasonably hardy, it is also slow to bolt and is best sown in late summer for an autumn crop.

Mizuna

Almost certainly Chinese in origin, but developed in Japan. It forms a bushy plant of dark green feathery leaves, with a mild mustardy flavour.

Mibuna

Another variety developed in Japan. **Mibuna** forms an attractive plant with a spray of long narrow leaves. These are mild-flavoured, although usually stronger than **Mizuna**.

Green-in-the-snow

One of the first Oriental mustards to be introduced to the West. Plants have dark green jagged-edged leaves and a peppery flavour. This variety is very vigorous and exceptionally hardy.

Giant Red

A mustard green with handsome red-tinted leaves. When mature, the plants can have leaves up to 60cm (2ft) long, or you can sow this variety closely and use the seedlings for cut greens.

PARSNIPS
Pastinaca sativa (Umbelliferae)

Cultivated parsnips evolved from the wild parsnips native to much of Europe and Central Asia. They appear to have been a staple crop in Northern Europe in the Middle Ages, but by the 16th century had lost much of their popularity, and on mainland Europe were most likely to be used as animal food. However, they have consistently remained popular in the UK, where some old varieties still exist. The roots are very sweet, and they are traditionally served baked or roasted, also in soups and stews.

Parsnips will grow well on most soils, although long-rooted types do best on deep, light soils. They do not need much feeding. Seeds are slow to germinate, so it is most successful to wait until soil is warm in mid to late spring before sowing, for harvesting in the autumn and winter. Plants are hardy and it is generally considered that frost improves the roots' flavour.

Parsnips are biennial, producing umbels of tiny flowers in the summer after sowing. These are insect-pollinated, and crossing can occur between varieties and with wild parsnips growing in field margins.

Hollow Crown / Guernsey / Large Sugar
A favourite old variety, much cultivated in the Channel Islands and the UK at the beginning of the 19th century – and probably long before. It has smooth white roots which grow up to 36cm (15in) long, and sweet white flesh. It will yield heavily in deep beds; and stores well.

The Student
Try this one for its history alone! Some of the first written records of parsnips describe the plants growing in a Bishop's garden in Cirencester, England, in the 9th century. This variety was selected in 1860 from wild seedlings at the Royal Agricultural College in Cirencester, so it could be closely related to those earliest strains. Thick tapering roots grow to 50cm (20in), and are extremely mild and sweet. It is good baked and in soups

Tender and True
Named after a popular song in the 19th century, this variety is worth growing for its fine-grained sweet flesh and heavily tapered roots which are almost without cores.

PEAS

Pisum sativum var *sativum (Leguminosae)*

Peas were one of the earliest vegetables to be cultivated. They probably originated in the Near East but spread early on through Asia and Europe. Pea seeds have been found in Bronze and Iron Age settlements in Northern Europe, and peas are mentioned by Greek and Roman writers.

The first peas were tough and starchy, and were dried for storage then cooked for a long time in soups and dishes such as 'pease pudding' popular in England in the Middle Ages. Some small black or grey drying peas, usually distinguishable by their purple flowers, are still cultivated today. Shelling or podding peas, eaten fresh, do not seem to have appeared until the 16th century. These first podding peas had smooth round seeds and were very hardy, and gardeners still use their descendants for early sowings. They were followed by the much sweeter but less hardy wrinkle-seeded peas which are now the most commonly cultivated.

The other type of peas are sugar, mangetout or snow peas, in which the entire pods are eaten, usually when they are small and the peas are immature. In some varieties (now called 'snap' peas) the pod wall becomes very thick, fleshy and sweet, and the pods can be eaten when the peas have swelled. Although sugar peas have become fashionable in recent years, they are not new, but are the main type of pea traditionally eaten in China and much of Asia. Several European varieties were described in Vilmorin's *The Vegetable Garden* in 1885.

Peas may be tall or dwarf: tall peas are likely to be traditional varieties, because plant breeding has made modern varieties low growing for ease of mechanical harvesting. Tall varieties tend to be more prolific and crop over a long period, but the plants are more trouble to support.

Peas are cool-weather crops, and prefer moisture-retentive soil containing plenty of organic matter. Extra feeding is rarely needed because bacteria associated with the roots of legumes have the ability to utilise atmospheric nitrogen. The plants must be supported with sticks, trellis or netting, and watering is important when they start to flower and pod. Successive sowings can be made from early spring to early summer to provide a continuous harvest.

Flowers are self-pollinating and crossing is usually minimal as long as varieties are not grown directly alongside one another. They are very easy to save for seed.

PODDING / GARDEN PEAS

Champion of England
Bred in 1843 as **Fairford's Champion of England**, this midseason wrinkled variety produces long pods containing 8–10 peas. Growing up to 2m (6ft) tall, it gives good crops in dry and wet conditions, and will even yield reasonably in high heat and humidity or semi-drought.

Prince Albert
The most popular variety of English pea in America during the mid-19th century, grown in England since the 1830s. This tall, wrinkle-seeded variety was grown by Thomas Jefferson in his gardens at Monticello, Virginia. Sow in January for cropping in May, then save some seeds from this crop and sow them in July for a September harvest.

Thomas Laxton
This semi-dwarf, smooth-seeded pea is a direct descendant of the original 19th century Laxton pea. 75 cm (30in) vines produce dark green square-ended pods with large dark peas, which do particularly well in cool climates. These peas are excellent for freezing.

Kelvedon Wonder
An old English variety, deep green pods containing sweet wrinkle-seeded peas are produced abundantly on short plants about 45cm (18in) tall. Sow this variety from early spring for successive cropping.

Ne Plus Ultra
A tall garden pea from the 1840s which was very popular in the UK in the 1860s and 1870s. Peas grow on white flowered vines to 2m (6ft) tall; long rounded pods contain 7 very sweet, juicy and uniform peas in each. Very useful as a late pea, sowing in April to crop from July to September, this variety appears to be mildew resistant.

Epicure
A very tasty sweet wrinkled pea that can grow to 3m (10ft) tall, sometimes even higher. It produces well filled pods that can be picked for many weeks.

Alderman / Tall Telephone
First mentioned in British seed catalogues in 1891, this is a good late main crop variety; large smooth-seeded pods are easy to pick from 2m (6ft) vines, and peas have a good flavour.

Roi des Conserves
This very old French midseason variety has round peas that really do store well. Use them fresh or for drying.

Magnum Bonum
This Victorian variety can grow to 2.5m (8ft) in good conditions. It is very productive over a long period, and has beautiful large white flowers. The peas have a good flavour and may have better resistance to pea moth damage than many other varieties.

Östgötaärt
One of several old local Swedish varieties and landraces of tall pea. It is very high yielding and pods are filled with tasty large flat peas.

Segner von Reidt
An old Austrian pea variety which grows to 1.5m (5ft) and produces masses of largish pods. Austria has a long tradition of pea growing, but few named varieties. Most taller varieties are endangered.

SUGAR / MANGETOUT PEAS

Golden Sweet

A beautiful, ancient, but still extremely rare pea from India with lemon-yellow edible pods. 2–2.5m (6–8ft) vines produce beautiful flowers in two shades of purple. The small peas are best eaten as young sugar peas, but are also good dried for soup, and the plants are definitely worth growing for their ornamental value. This variety may be one of those originally used by Mendel to study inheritance, in the experiments that created the basic foundations of genetics.

Carouby de Maussanne

This traditional French variety is exceptionally tasty. The plants grow very tall, from 2m (6ft), with long wide pods containing very sweet peas that can be picked for podding or eaten whole as mangetouts. Attractive flowers are violet-coloured.

Schweizer Riesen

Large, tender, tasty snow peas grow on purple flowered tall vines with purple leaf stipules. The peas are so sweet that dried pods have a sticky sweet syrup inside! This pea is a favourite Swiss heritage variety, perfect for cooler areas.

Chinese Snow

This is a beautiful and rare tall pea. It climbs to 3m (10ft), producing white flowers followed by sweet crunchy pods. Pick before the seeds get plump.

DRYING PEAS

Carlin

This drying pea dates back to Elizabethan times or earlier. It grows to 2m (6ft) tall, with attractive two-tone purple flowers. Seeds are small and brown, slightly mottled, and are traditionally eaten in the north east of England on Carlin Sunday, two weeks before Easter.

Blauwschokker / Blue Capucjin

This unique variety is a tasty and beautiful addition to any ornamental garden. Pinkish-violet flowers are followed by numerous purple-violet pods, filled with big sweet greenish-brown peas. These can be picked fresh but are best for drying.

Victorian red-podded

This variety grows 1.75–2m (5–6ft) tall, with two-tone red and purple flowers. Most pods are dark blue with some green. The dried peas have a very good flavour.

PEPPERS & CHILLIES
Capsicum annuum (Solanaceae)

Peppers are natives of tropical America, cultivated throughout Central and South America for thousands of years – they featured on ceramics dating back to 5000BC. When Columbus arrived in America in 1493 he thought that he had arrived in the spice-growing East Indies, and he took peppers back to Spain as substitutes for true pepper (*Piper nigrum*); the name persists. From Spain, peppers spread eastwards to East Africa, India and the Far East, where they were quickly adopted, giving rise to local varieties and the regional cooking we now consider typical: hot dishes of India, salads of Italy and paprikas of Hungary. It took much longer for peppers to be adopted in Northern Europe.

Most peppers grown here are *Capsicum annuum* species. These include sweet peppers and hot peppers or chillies. Some varieties of *C. pubescens* and *C. baccatum* are also in cultivation. The most familiar sweet peppers are the green, red or yellow bell peppers, and chillies are usually thought of as small, thin, red pods, but a much greater diversity exists. Fruits range from purple-black or brown to pale yellow; some are small, some large, some round, some heart-shaped, some almost square. The colour and shape of peppers do not indicate whether they are sweet or hot.

All peppers are grown as annuals in cool climates, and they need warm, light conditions and a fertile and moisture-retentive soil. In Northern Europe they are most reliably grown under cover. Sow seeds in early spring with some heat – they need temperatures over 20°C (68°F) to germinate.

Pepper flowers are self-pollinating, but cross-pollination by insects can occur. Much of the heat in chillies is in the seeds, so take care when extracting them; make sure the room is well ventilated, wear rubber gloves, and avoid touching your eyes.

SWEET PEPPERS

Large Sweet Spanish/ Bull Nose/ Large Bell / Sweet Mountain

Introduced to Europe in the 18th century via India and the US, these large fruits can be stuffed and pickled, but they are also delicious in salads and for frying. Four-lobed fruits ripen from green to scarlet, and have sweet thick flesh and slightly hot ribs, but the heat depends on growing conditions and only comes through in hotter climates.

Nardello / Jimmy Nardello's Sweet Frying

An excellent Italian frying pepper. Large heavy-cropping plants need to be tied or staked to support numerous long slender fruits which grow up to 20cm (8in) long. These peppers are strong at the green stage becoming very sweet when red. They are fantastic for pasta sauce.

Pimento

Thick-walled heart-shaped fruits are dark green, ripening to orange-red, and very sweet.

Manda / Yellow Bell

This Yugoslavian heirloom has been in cultivation for at least 200 years. A multiple-lobed sweet yellow bell pepper, it is great in salads or stuffed. The peppers appear above the foliage of the compact 60cm (2ft) plants, providing a very attractive display.

Hungarian Sweet Yellow / Sweet Banana

Hungary has a tradition of pepper breeding; this is one of the most commonly known varieties, and it is very reliable, producing heavy yields of attractive pointed yellow peppers about 15cm (6in) long.

Cece

An old Austrian variety which is still available commercially. Plants are tiny with a mass of very sweet yellow peppers. This variety is very similar to hard-to-find old Hungarian varieties with names such as Feherözon Paprika, and Ètkezesi Feher Húsú.

Sweet Cherry / Red Cherry

These tiny fruits look like children's sweets! They are very sweet, good for pickling, canning, or fresh for snacks and salads. Bushy 48 cm (20in) plants reliably bear very heavy yields of highly ornamental 3-4cm (1-1.5in) fruits.

Hot Peppers

Czechoslovakian Black

A highly-recommended ornamental pepper, medium hot, early, adaptable, attractive and tasty! Green foliage is veined purple, and lavender flowers are streaked white. 1m (3ft) plants bear medium-hot blunt ended conical fruits, red near the base of the bush and purple-black at the top. These need full sun to colour up effectively.

Hungarian Yellow Wax Hot / Hot Banana

An old Hungarian variety which is well adapted to cool and hotter climates. Long banana-shaped peppers turn from green through yellow to red; spicy, medium-hot, they are great fresh, pickled or canned.

Anaheim / Long Green Chillie

Cultivated in New Mexico for more than 300 years, these peppers are pale to medium bright green with long tapered pods. They need reliable and continuous sunshine to attain their full flavour, even under glass. Their heat ranges from mild to medium. **Red Anaheim** is sweetest, and pods are traditionally left on the bushy plant until they turn leathery, then dried in the sun to be ground into powder. **Green Anaheims** are good roasted and stuffed or peeled and made into sauces.

Long Red Cayenne

Small wrinkled pods are waxy dark green to crimson, curled, twisted and tapered. Bushy plants grow to 75cm (30in) tall. These small peppers are fiery hot, even when very small, perfect for drying.

Yellow Romanian / Karlo

This old European heirloom produces sweet and hot peppers about 12cm (5in) long and 5cm (2in) wide at the shoulder. They are particularly good for baking and stuffing, as well as in stews.

POTATOES
Solanum tuberosum (Solanaceae)

The homeland of potatoes is the Andes in South America, where many wild potato species still grow. There is evidence of their cultivation at least 2000 years ago, and it is likely they were grown for centuries before that. The varieties of potatoes traditionally grown are much more diverse in colour and shape, and their tolerance to different conditions and diseases much greater than our smooth oval red or white modern varieties. Many of these traditional varieties are still cultivated by Andean and Mexican farmers today.

Potatoes were taken back to Europe by the Spanish conquerors in the 16th century, but did not become popular for some time, partly because people suspected the tubers were poisonous, but also because the plants failed to yield reliably in the long cool northern days. The Irish were among the first to make significant use of the potato, and despite its ancient history in South America, the potato only went to North America with early Irish settlers.

Potatoes weren't grown widely in Europe until the end of the 18th century, but they then spread rapidly. Today they are grown around the world and, in terms of quantity, are the fourth most important crop in the world, after wheat, maize and rice.

Although many potatoes do produce viable true seed in the round green fruit formed on the foliage, each seed produces a plant with different characteristics. To obtain plants that are true to type you must usually propagate from small 'seed' potatoes.

To yield well, potatoes need a fertile soil and plenty of moisture. They are frost tender, but in cool climates the growing season can be extended by starting the tubers into growth indoors in early spring until their shoots have developed, then planting the sprouting tubers into the ground in mid to late spring. Plants are usually earthed up or mulched during growth to prevent the greening of tubers that are pushed to the surface.

The problem with saving tubers for replanting is that potatoes are very susceptible to virus diseases, which are carried over in the tubers and can affect the growth of future crops. Seed tubers are grown commercially in areas where there is a low risk of infection, and they are rigorously inspected. Small quantities can also be produced by growing potatoes in aphid-proof tunnels as it is usually aphids that spread the infections.

Belle de Fontenay

An old French variety, introduced in the 1880s, valued for its fine taste and waxy texture which makes it ideal for potato salads. The yellow tubers are smooth and slightly curved. Unfortunately this variety is highly susceptible to blight and virus infections.

Witch Hill / Snowdrop

This variety is particularly important in potato history: in 1907 potato wart disease became a major problem in parts of the UK, and **Snowdrop** was discovered to be completely resistant, and therefore of vital importance. It is a smooth white kidney-shaped potato, with shallow eyes and snow-white flesh. Floury and well flavoured, it retains its colour in cooking and storage.

Lumpers

This was the main Irish variety before the potato famine of 1845. Dating back to 1808, the name probably came about because it was brought to Ireland by the 'lumpers', itinerant labourers who worked in the lumber yards of the London dockyards. Opinions are divided about its taste: contemporary records by visiting Englishmen denounced it as 'scarcely fit for pigs', but modern opinion suggests it is a fine, tasty, floury potato. However, beware the blight!

Ratte / Cornichon / Asperges/ Saucisse de Lyon

This popular old potato from France produces very long pale slender tubers. They are reasonably smooth with firm dark yellow flesh which keeps an excellent texture when cooked. They have a distinctive chestnut flavour, which is excellent cold as well as hot. Ideal for salads, these are often, particularly in their homeland, grown as an alternative to **Pink Fir Apple**. **Ratte** is however, difficult to grow; it is prone to blight, and virus affects a significant proportion of the seed.

Pink Fir Apple

First popularised in the 1880s, this has recently become popular again in the UK, particularly as a salad potato, and in France it is used as one of the best varieties for French fries although **Ratte** (*see above*) is an easier shape to handle. Tubers are long, pink and rather knobby with waxy yellow flesh. They stay firm when cooked, and their flavour is wonderful, but they are not easy to grow, and are susceptible to blight and other diseases.

Edzell Blue

Originally raised in Scotland, the knobbly oval tubers of this early maincrop variety have beautiful blue/purple skin which contrasts with their snow-white flesh. Very floury and delicious, **Edzell Blue** have a tendency to disintegrate if boiled, so they are best steamed or microwaved.

Naglerner Kipfel / German Fingerling

This potato is a speciality of Austria, and has a characteristic taste and solid texture. Tubers are elongated and slightly moon shaped, with yellow flesh and yellowish skin. It is interesting to note that Hitler outlawed this potato because its yield did not keep up with standard varieties producing more mass for the 'war effort'.

Vitelotte Noire / La Nigresse

The skin and flesh of this cylindrical potato is a deep blueish purple, and the flesh doesn't lose its colour when cooked. Blue potatoes come from the Andes, but they were introduced into Provence some 200 years ago. **La Nigresse** is a typical peasant cultivar of the region, and the Provençal people consider it part of their heritage. This is very good for salads, or as a decorative purée.

Irene

A traditional Dutch variety, this early maincrop potato is oval, pale-skinned with bright red eyes and yellow flesh. It cooks swiftly, has excellent flavour, produces reliably and appears to be disease resistant.

Blaue Odenwalder

One of the oldest known German 'blue' potatoes, purple-skinned with white flesh, this maincrop variety produces reliably under most conditions. Potatoes are floury and delicious steamed, boiled or mashed. The flavour is very good, but this variety is becoming increasingly rare.

Flourball

Red-skinned, smooth round to oval tubers have deep eyes and white flesh, sometimes tinged with pink. **Flourball** is a late cropper, resistant to blight and immune to potato wart disease. Floury, with a pleasant strong flavour, tubers store well.

Skerry Blue

A late maincrop potato from Ireland, introduced there from Scotland before 1860. Violet-skinned, with white flesh, this has historic popularity as it was deemed to be blight resistant. In fact it escaped the worst of the potato blight in 1865 because it is such a late variety, and it does grow on well after a blight attack. It has a slightly insipid flavour, but has a good colour when baked, steamed or boiled, and it crops productively.

RADISHES
Raphanus sativus (Cruciferae)

Although their exact origins are uncertain, radishes have been cultivated since ancient times. They were grown in China over 2000 years ago, and in Egypt workers on the pyramids were given them in their rations along with garlic and onions. The Ancient Greeks had radishes made of gold as a dedication to Apollo at his temple in Delphi.

In Europe radishes are mainly grown for their roots, and these have been eaten raw as appetisers for several hundred years. Most familiar today are the small red, white or pink radishes which are harvested young for salads. The various types of large radish are less well known in Europe, but are valued vegetables in China and Japan, used for pickling and cooking as well as raw.

Long white 'mooli' radishes can grow over 60cm (2ft) long. They are generally grown for autumn and early winter harvesting, but most available varieties are modern hybrids. However, some traditional hardy Chinese and Spanish winter radishes can still be found.

Radishes may also be cultivated for their immature pods, traditionally used fresh for salads or for pickling, also for their young leaves. Small salad radishes are quick growing, and you need to make successive sowings from spring through summer for continuous supply. They need plenty of moisture and should not be overcrowded or good roots will not develop. Most types of mooli radish are best sown in mid summer for autumn harvesting as they tend to bolt in lengthening days. Winter radishes are sown in late summer, and can be left in the ground over winter in all but the coldest areas. Radishes may be annual or biennial, and often produce very tall flower stalks which need staking. Insect pollinated, they will cross with other radish varieties.

Summer / Autumn Radishes

Wood's Frame
On the English National List until 1984, this radish has a long pink tapering root which is used when it is about 6–9cm (2–3in) long. It was originally bred for forcing in frames outside for th early market. The flavour is very strong.

French Golden
As these plants mature the roots appear to change from red to yellow. These are very crunchy and juicy, not too peppery. Leave some plants to bolt and produce pods which are very good to eat raw, with a flavour just like the roots.

French Breakfast
This traditional-looking rosy scarlet radish has a white tip, and its crisp white flesh is mildly piquant. Cold-hardy, it can be planted from early spring to autumn. The green tops and roots can be pickled or cooked.

Long White Icicle / Lady's Finger
A mild-flavoured crunchy white variety with tapering roots up to 12cm (5in) long. Although best harvested small, it stays crisp and mild if left in the ground to grow large. Sow this one from early summer on, as it is tolerant of heat and drought, with excellent crunchy texture and slightly spicy flavour.

Rote Reisen von Aspern
Large round fast-growing radishes used to be available in a variety of colours and forms from local gardeners all over Austria. This commercial red variety is still widely available, and Viennese gardeners are still selling their own unnamed varieties. The radishes are very sweet, tender and crisp.

Winter Radishes

China Rose
This winter radish was very popular at the end of the 19th century. It has extremely pungent firm white flesh; the roots are half long and bright carmine red.

Round Black Spanish
This autumn or winter-keeping variety has large black-skinned roots with firm white pungent flesh. Grow these primarily for winter storage as they keepwell all winter, particularly when stored in moist sand. Black radishes were grown widely in Northern Europe in the 18th century.

Long Black Spanish
Another excellent winter storage variety. Cylindrical roots grow to about 20cm (8in). They are black skinned with crisp white tasty flesh.

Violet de Gournay
This radish came originally from the market garden region of Bray in Northern France, and has been grown for over a century. It is similar to Long Black Spanish, but has a deep purple skin and is slightly more conical in shape.

PODDING RADISHES

München Bier

This old variety is grown for its edible pods, 5cm (2in) long and stringless. They are quite sweet and juicy, good raw or cooked. You can also sow in spring, summer and autumn and use the long white roots during the winter.

Rat's Tail

This radish from South Asia is traditionally grown for its edible pods, and has been known in Europe for over 100 years. It does not form a swollen root, but goes straight to flower. Blooms are followed by long slender purplish pods – usually about 3 months after sowing. Pick them young, at about 10cm (4in), as they tend to become fibrous and hard if they grow to their full size of 20cm (8in) or more. They are delicious raw in salads, and also very good pickled.

SALSIFY & SCORZONERA
Tragopogon porrifolius & Scorzonera hispanica (Compositae)

Salsify and scorzonera are very similar root vegetables, both native to Southern Europe. It is said that they were developed by Italian gardeners, but both vegetables have been grown in Northern Europe for centuries although they have never become more than a minor commercial crop. You can only find unnamed types and a few traditional varieties.

Salsify is a biennial plant with a long creamy brown root and narrow leaves. The roots have a delicate flavour, sometimes said to resemble oysters, hence the plant's other name of 'vegetable oyster'. Scorzonera is a perennial plant with long black-skinned roots tasting similar to salsify. Young blanched shoots and flower buds of both vegetables can be used in salads or stir-fries.

Both plants grow best on deep light soil. Seed is usually sown in spring for autumn and winter harvest, or leave scorzonera roots in the ground to thicken up for the next year.

Sandwich Island Salsify

Dull white roots grow to about 25cm (10in) long, and taper to a point – they look like slender parsnips. Flesh is creamy-white. Leave **Sandwich Island** in the ground until after the first frost, as this makes the roots more tender. This variety has been grown in Europe since the end of the 19th century.

Géante Noire de Russe / Russian Giant Scorzonera

Very long cylindrical black-skinned roots can grow to 45cm (18in). This variety is the most prized by European cooks for soups and stews, or baked or creamed. If the roots are too thin or forked to harvest, leave the plants in the ground until the following year to thicken.

SKIRRET
Sium sisarum (Umbelliferae)

Skirret is an old root vegetable whose origins are unclear. The Roman Emperor Tiberius is reputed to have introduced it to Italy in the 1st century AD, and it has been cultivated in Northern Europe for many centuries. It is rarely seen today.

Skirret is a hardy perennial, each plant having a bundle of long thin ridged whitish roots which are very sweet and tender when cooked, although they may have a woody core. Plants thrive in moisture-retentive soil, and are easy to propagate from seed sown in spring or from offsets of mature plants.

Roots are ready for harvest in autumn and can be left in the ground in winter unless frosts are very severe. Although named varieties are not available, you could select your own strain by repeatedly propagating from plants with the largest and the most tender roots.

SEA KALE
Crambe maritima (Cruciferae)

The sea kale grown by gardeners is little removed from the wild sea kale which grows along the coasts of northern Europe. It is a hardy perennial plant, grown for its young spring shoots, which are traditionally blanched by covering them with earthenware pots. For centuries people living along the south coast of England would harvest the wild crop and sell it at market, and it was cultivated in English gardens at the beginning of the 18th century. However, the crop has only ever really been popular in a few areas, despite the fact it is easy to g row and delicious.

Plants are normally raised from root cuttings or 'thongs' which give plants that are true to type, but you can raise plants from seed and select the strongest to make a permanent bed.

Lilywhite
One of the few named sea kale selections, this old variety has pure green leaves without the purple tinge of the common type. It is a heavy cropper with well flavoured shoots.

SPINACH

Spinacea oleracea (Chenopodiaceae)

Spinach originated in Central and Southwestern Asia, first cultivated by the Persians, probably around the 6th century AD, and a century later by the Chinese. It was taken by the Arabs to Spain, and had become a familiar vegetable as far north as England by the end of the 16th century. Lightly cooked, it is a valuable ingredient in many traditional European dishes.

Spinach is a quick-growing annual. Old varieties were classified as round-seeded, usually used for summer crops, and prickly-seeded, which were reputedly hardier and sown for winter crops. Spinach plants need rich fertile soil, and plenty of moisture; they tend to bolt very quickly if grown in hot and dry conditions.

New Zealand spinach (*Tetragonia expansa*) is a half-hardy perennial often used as a substitute for true spinach. It is native to Australia and New Zealand, and was taken to Kew Gardens in England in the late 18th century by botanist Joseph Banks, who was on board Captain Cook's ship on its voyage around the world. In cool climates it is grown as an annual, but it readily self-seeds; it is more tolerant of heat and drought than true spinach.

Norfolk

Originally from Quebec, this hardy strain is recommended for autumn sowing. Tidy compact leaves have lacy edges and they stay tender and well-flavoured for cutting all winter long. Although this is probably the best strain of all for cold climates, it is currently in danger of extinction.

Viroflay

One of the most important varieties, introduced in the 1880s and much used for breeding modern hybrids. The large leaves are very low in acid and stay tender even when very large.

Broad Leaved Prickly

Another excellent late autumn and winter spinach, a very strong variety that can withstand some frost, maintaining tender deep green leaves.

Strawberry Spinach

This plant comes from Southern Europe. Coarsely toothed spear-shaped leaves bear spikes of dense clusters of tiny green flowers which turn into edible small red fruits. They don't have a very strong flavour but can be added to salad as an unusual decoration, or boiled or steamed.

Münsterlander Scharfsämiger

This unusual old variety of spinach from Northern Germany has very deep green leaves which stay tender even in heat, and withstand some frost.

SPINACH BEET / SWISS CHARD / LEAF BEET
Beta vulgaris (Chenopodiaceae)

Like beetroot, chards and spinach beet are descended from wild beet, but these vegetables have been selected for their leaves rather than for their roots. Chards have broad stems and midribs which are usually white, although there are some striking red, pink and yellow forms, all considered equally ancient; Aristotle praised a red-stemmed chard in around 350BC. They are handsome plants, equally at home in the ornamental garden. Stems are usually cut from the leaves and eaten as a separate vegetable.

Spinach beet has narrow green midribs and it is used like true spinach. Chard and spinach beet prefer rich moist soil. They are usually sown in mid to late spring for harvesting throughout the summer and autumn.

They are biennial plants and will stand until spring where winters are not too severe. They can then be cropped until they run to seed. Plants are wind-pollinated and will cross with each other, and with beetroot.

Lucullus

This old variety was named after the Roman general Lucullus who was renowned for magnificent banquets. It produces well flavoured greens prolifically throughout the growing season, and may be encouraged to overwinter if the base of the plants are mulched. The foliage is pale green and ruffled.

Argentata

This vigorous Italian heirloom has silvery white midribs, and deep green savoyed leaves. Although less hardy than some varieties, its flavour is delicate and delicious.

Five Colour Silver Beet / Rainbow Chard

When people first see this variety they don't believe it can be an old variety, as the colours are so vivid they look as though they have been carefully developed in the lab! But coloured varieties of chard were grown in ancient times. The fantastic mix of colours – midribs can be red, pink, orange, creamy-silver and yellow – makes this a perfect ornamental plant, and the flavour is very good.

Ruby Red / Rhubarb Chard

The tender rhubarb-like ruby red stalks and dark green heavily crumpled leaves with dark red veins make this another very ornamental variety. It has the mildest flavour of all chards.

Perpetual Spinach / Spinach Beet

Most British gardens grow this variety, which has small dark green leaves over a long season, tolerating most weather conditions and almost never bolting. Plants look and taste much like spinach although they are slightly coarser in texture.

SQUASHES, MARROWS & PUMPKINS
Cucurbita spp. (Cucurbitaceae)

The names used for this varied group of vegetables are often confusing, and referring to their botanical species does not always help. Summer squash are all those which are usually used fresh from the vine. The familiar long green marrows are a type of summer squash, and courgettes are small immature marrows. Other types include the bright orange crookneck squash which were among the first vegetables brought to Europe from America in the 17th century. Most summer squash belong to the species *C. pepo*.

Winter squash will develop a hard skin if allowed to mature on the vine, and will usually store for many months. Pumpkin tends to be the name associated with the winter squashes that are large, round and orange, but sometimes all winter squash are called pumpkins. Many of the winter squash grown in Northern Europe belong to the species *C. maxima*, but some are *C. pepo* and some *C. moschata* or *C. mixta*, although these last two types are rarely grown in Northern Europe as they prefer considerably warmer climates.

Squash are one of the oldest staple crops of America, where a vast diversity could be found, used for food but also for bowls and kitchen utensils as well as animal food. In Europe there are a few traditional varieties, developed in the 18th and 19th centuries, particularly in France, but relatively few of the diverse American varieties are available.

Squash are quick-growing frost tender annuals. They need a very rich moisture-retentive soil and a sunny site to flourish. Sow seeds outside when all danger of frost is past, or indoors in pots with heat. The more you pick summer squash, the more fruits they will produce over a long period; let winter squash mature on the vine and bring them into storage before the first frosts.

Squash flowers are insect pollinated. Although varieties of different species do not cross-pollinate crossing readily occurs between varieties of the same species. However, flowers are relatively easy to hand pollinate and isolate for saving seed (*see Chapter 5, pages 90–97*).

SUMMER SQUASHES, MARROWS & COURGETTES
Cucurbita pepo

Long Green Trailing / Long Green Striped
Listed in European catalogues in the 1880s, this is a traditional marrow variety producing large fruits of dark green with paler stripes. Very tasty, this is extremely easy to grow and stores well without going soft.

Yellow Crookneck
Crooknecks are among the oldest varieties of summer squash, a type that the Spaniards brought back to Europe in the 17th century. Yellow bulb-shaped fruit, growing on open bushy plants, have a narrow curved neck, and the skin gets warty as fruits get larger. Creamy-white flesh is good for steaming and frying, and excellent grilled.

Ronde de Nice

An old French heirloom with fantastic flavoured light green globes of fruit. The skin is very delicate, so you are unlikely ever to see these on shop shelves, but they're one of the nicest for gardeners and cooks – flesh is custardy smooth and rich. Bushy plants are fast-growing and productive.

Cocozelle / Italian Vegetable Marrow

Long cylindrical courgettes have smooth flesh beneath a green and white striped skin. The 58cm (2ft) bushes of this Italian heirloom produce fruits which are delicious picked tiny and eaten whole, otherwise wait until they reach about 17cm (7in) and steam or grill them. They have a pleasantly nutty flavour.

Tromboncino

This unusual variety produces long curved courgettes with a bell at the flower end. They will grow up to 1m (3ft) long, keeping a good flavour and texture from small to large. The plants are very vigorous climbers, attractive if grown over an arch or frame, or they can trail on the ground.

Acoma

Originally from the north of Mexico, the fruits of this old variety of marrow are very large ovals striped dark and pale green. The skin is thin and tender, and the flesh ranges from white to pale yellow, depending on size and maturity. Although each plant will only produce about 4 fruits, each weighs 4–6kg (8-10lb), and they will keep for several months.

Delicata

Introduced to Europe from the US, where it is commonly known as the **Peanut Squash**, medium short vines bear oblong cream-coloured squash with dark green and orange stripes and splashes. The flesh on 1kg (2lb) fruits is firm textured and incredibly sweet. Although a summer squash, **Delicata** can be stored for at least 4 months.

Verte de Milan

One of the most productive old courgette varieties. Fruits are dark green, almost black, with excellent flavour. Keep picking the plants to ensure a steady supply for 6-8 weeks.

Spaghetti Marrow

Apparently this old variety originated in Manchuria, although most spaghetti marrows are modern varieties, so be careful when choosing. White fruits on very vigorous plants turn deep yellow as they mature, and grow to about 30cm (12in), typically weighing 1–3kg (2–6lb). They store exceptionally well, for 6 months or more without deterioration. When cooked, the flesh comes apart in long strands like spaghetti, and many people use it in recipes instead of the pasta.

Yellow Custard

This old variety was very popular with gardeners at the end of the 19th century. Medium-sized scalloped orange fruits have sweet orange flesh, great for grilling.

Pale Green Pattypan

Attractive white star shaped fruits turn pale green as they ripen. The young fruits can be eaten sliced and steamed or fried like courgettes. Mature fruits are good stuffed or baked.

Melonette Jaspée de Vendée

This old French variety produces a good number of yellowish-orange fruits that look like little melons, down to the way their skin is marked with masses of little light coloured cracks like the netting on melons. The flesh is very sweet and orange, delicious baked and stuffed. These squash keep for several months.

WINTER SQUASHES / PUMPKINS

Cucurbita pepo

Mandan

Originally grown by the Mandan Native American tribe, plants are bush-type at first, but then runners appear which produce a second crop of attractive fruits, each 1.5–2kg (3–4lb). The skin is slightly warty, creamy white with yellow stripes and mottling. As this variety doesn't grow well in hot humid areas, it is perfect for the Northern European climate.

Lady Godiva

This is a naked-seeded variety, the seeds do not have a shell-like coating around them, and it is grown primarily for the seeds which are eaten dried, but the flesh is also tasty. Pick these when their skin is entirely yellow, remove and wash the seeds and dry them at a temperature of 18-20°C (64-68°F).

Cucurbita maxima

Pink Banana

An old Native American variety with very long banana shaped fruits 30–120cm (12–50in) long. Plants are very vigorous and productive, each plant can produce numerous large fruits from 5–20kg (10–50lb), with skins that ripen to an attractive rose-pink colour. The flesh is bright orange and fairly sweet.

Olive

Widely cultivated in France in the 19th century, in *The Vegetable Garden* (1885) Vilmorin suggests that this squash derives its name from the shape and colour of the fruits, which resemble huge unripe olives. This is a good vigorous and productive variety, but it is rather late to mature so does not always ripen fully for storage. The golden yellow flesh is tasty with a pleasant texture.

Green Hubbard / Hubbard / True Hubbard

This is the original hubbard squash, which came to Europe via North America from the West Indies in the 18th century. Tough-skinned pointed orange-green fruits weigh 22–35kg (10–15lb), and golden yellow flesh is dry and mealy with a fantastic flavour. These store well throughout the winter, keeping their texture and flavour.

Queensland Blue

Popularised in Australia, extremely productive sprawling vines produce quantities of striking blue-green fruits up to 15lb (25kg). These store exceptionally well. The flesh is moist and nutty flavoured.

Turk's Turban

Grow these primarily for ornamental interest, although the flesh is particularly good in soups, if rather insipid otherwise. Small flattened fruits are up to 12in (28cm) across. When mature, the tough skins are orange with an orange-red, cream and green 'acorn' top. They really do look like their namesake.

Rouge Vif d'Etampes / Cinderella

This French heirloom is a classically beautiful, oblate and deeply ribbed pumpkin, a striking orange-red colour when fully ripe. Each plant produces up to 4 pumpkins 4–20kg (10–45lb) each. They have very good flavoured flesh, will store for several months and they are ideal for carving into lanterns!

Arbuzik Borodavachatkaya

The small warted fruits of this unusual Russian squash look like ornamental gourds, but they are delicious to eat, with firm sweet orange flesh.

SWEDES
Brassica napus (Cruciferae)

Swedes are a comparatively recent root vegetable – probably originating in Southern Germany in the 16th or 17th century and spreading north and west. It is sometimes said that a swede is a cross between a cabbage and a turnip. The American name 'rutabaga' comes from the Swedish *rotbagga* meaning ram's root.

Relatively hardy, swedes do best in cool moist conditions, hence their relative popularity in the most northerly European countries. In Scotland they quickly displaced the previously widely-grown turnips to become part of traditional winter fare.

Sow swede seeds in early summer on light fertile soils, and roots will be ready for use by early autumn. They can be left in the ground for several months unless winters are extremely harsh, although early maturing varieties can become woody and coarse if left for too long. Traditional varieties tend to be hardier, and have more flavour than modern varieties.

Plants are biennial, flowers forming the second year. They are insect pollinated, and crossing can occur between different varieties.

Champion Purple Top
This very large purple topped yellow swede was a popular exhibition variety in the middle of the 19th century. Globe-shaped roots have excellent textured sweet orange flesh.

Devon Champion
This attractive round midseason swede is also purple topped with yellow-orange flesh. It was probably grown in the 1930s and has been maintained by a small seed company in the West of England. It is now valued for its superior flavour over modern varieties.

Bjursäs
A traditional Swedish variety with juicy whitish flesh and an excellent flavour. It is small, with sparse foliage; the root is slightly elongated and the neck continues as a stem. This variety is not high yielding, but worth growing for texture and taste.

Bangholm Fenix
A traditional Danish variety, grown throughout Scandinavia, the flesh of this round red-topped swede ranges from orange to purplish-red. Flavour is good and this variety can be harvested from autumn through winter without becoming tough and woody.

SWEETCORN
Zea mays (Gramineae)

Maize or corn has its origins in tropical America, where it has been cultivated for thousands of years, spreading to North America via Native American tribes and also cultivated there for millennia. Corn was a vitally important crop for Native Americans, one of their staple foods, along with beans and squashes, and they developed local or tribal varieties *(see page 56),* some of which were imbued with sacred significance. Maize was brought back to Spain by Columbus in the 16th century, where it quickly became accepted as a cereal crop, but it only developed into the vegetable sweetcorn we know today in the second half of the 19th century.

Corn falls into several categories: flour corns have soft kernels; flint or dent corn is harder; popcorn has a floury kernel and a hard outer layer. All types can be eaten on the cob when young, but varieties developed specially for sweetcorn are sweetest and most palatable. Few traditional American corns will ripen in Northern European gardens, and most available sweetcorn varieties are F1 hybrids, but there are a few open-pollinated varieties that will do well in short growing seasons.

Sweetcorn prefers well-drained and reasonably fertile soil. It is frost tender and needs temperatures of over 10°C (50°F) to germinate, and in short-season areas must be started off indoors with heat. Cobs are ready to harvest when the tassel turns brown and when the kernels exude a milky juice. Pick traditional varieties just before use as they quickly lose their sweetness in storage.

Sweetcorn is wind and insect pollinated, and readily crosses with other varieties. It is best to set plants in blocks to help pollination, and for seed saving you will need to isolate varieties by about 800 metres (half a mile) or bag heads and pollinate by hand. The problems of crossing, and the large number of plants needed to maintain a healthy strain, mean that saving sweetcorn varieties for seed is not easy *(see Chapter 5, pages 90–97).*

Golden Bantam
This is the standard yellow sweetcorn for home gardeners, a favourite variety since the beginning of the century when it arrived in Northern Europe from the US. Plump sweet golden kernels form on 17cm (7in) ears on plants which grow to 2m (6^1/2ft) tall.

Mandan Red
This variety is best roasted. Plants are very short, with up to six 15cm (6in) ears per plant. Mandan Red is a pre-Columbian landrace which has been preserved by the Mandan Indians. It grows better in cooler climates than most corns.

Hooker's Sweet / Indian
First grown by Ira Hooker in the1920s in Washington, 1.4m (5ft) plants produce very fine tasting white sweetcorn whose 12–17cm (5–7in) ears mature blue-black. This variety is superb quality and very attractive, but it may not ripen in short-season areas.

**Black Aztec / Black Mexican /
Mexican Sweet / Black Iroquois**

This extremely hardy corn dates to pre-Columbian times. It starts out snowy-white, ripens to purple, then blackish-blue. It can be eaten as a fresh sweetcorn at the white stage, but is most often dried to produce a sweet blue-green corn meal.

Country Gentleman

Introduced in the US in 1890, this corn is unusual as the kernels do not grow in rows, but appear all over the cob. Flavour is excellent, and appearance interesting, but it needs sun and moisture, and may not ripen well in northern areas.

TOMATOES
Lycopersicon esculentum (Solanaceae)

Native to South America, tomatoes were probably first domesticated in Mexico and Central America. They were taken to Europe by Columbus in the 16th century, where they were at first regarded as poisonous, and grown solely as ornamental plants. By the end of the 18th century they were widely used in cooking and salads, and they have been popular ever since.

The early Italian name for tomato, *pomo d'oro* or golden apple, suggests that the first tomatoes in Europe were yellow or orange. Tomato colours range from yellow through orange, pink and red, with some that are almost brown or black, and some that are striped or splashed with a contrasting colour. Tomatoes also vary hugely in size, from minute currant tomatoes (*L. pimpinellifolium*) to enormous beefsteak varieties. They also show some variation in leaf shape, and in temperature and disease tolerance. These variations exist principally among the many traditional and heritage varieties.

Tomatoes are frost tender and need long warm summers to flourish. They are grown as half-hardy annuals in cool climates, and may do best in a glasshouse or polytunnel. Seeds generally need temperatures around 15°C (50°F) to germinate, so they are usually started off inside with some heat, for transplanting in early summer. Plants need a fertile moisture-retentive soil with plenty of organic matter.

Catalogues usually classify tomato varieties as determinate or indeterminate. Determinate varieties are bush types, which produce one crop rather than a prolonged harvest. Indeterminate or cordon types grow on long vines and need staking; if the side shoos that form on them are removed these varieties crop over a long period. All tomatoes are sweetest when grown in full sun, but most varieties will produce a good tasty crop even in cool areas.

Tomatoes self-pollinate and in most varieties cross-pollination is negligible, which makes seed saving simple. Even where cross-pollination might occur in older varieties, it is easy to cover flower trusses to isolate them (*see Chapter 5, pages 90–97*).

Tomatillos are the ancestors of tomatoes, still found wild in much of Central America. They need a warmer climate than tomatoes.

CHERRY / CURRANT TOMATOES

Broad Ripple Yellow Currant

Originally found growing in a crack in a pavement in downtown Indianapolis in the US, these tiny yellow tomatoes are extremely sweet and packed with flavour. Rampant bushy vines need at least 1m (3ft) between them as they grow very vigorously, producing numerous fruits on short trusses. These appear quite late in the season and will ripen readily off the vine.

Green Grape

Although most catalogues refer to this as a heritage variety, this is not strictly true: it was developed by crossing the heirloom **Yellow Pear** with the old-fash-ioned variety **Evergreen**. This very unusual variety produces tiny green fruits on weedy looking bushes. The sweet fruits turn a different shade of green to indicate ripeness, and are incredibly full of flavour. This variety needs continuous sun for fullest sweet ripeness, but will thrive in fairly arid conditions. It is worth growing for its fantastic sweet and tangy taste.

Yellow Pear

Yellow pear-shaped fruits are very low in acid, and have pleased gardeners in Europe since the late 1800s. Sweet and juicy, and easy to grow in most conditions, these fruits would be worth growing for their good colour and shape alone. **Yellow Pear** needs staking.

Riesentraube

The big bushy plants of this German heritage variety bear distinctive red pear-shaped fruits in large clusters of 20–30 fruits per group. The plants require little care, and still produce prolifically in uncertain sunshine. An excellent salad tomato, and great for snacks.

Red Pear

First grown before 1865, vigorous bushy plants produce masses of small pear-shaped fruits all summer long. Excellent for bottling.

RED TOMATOES

Harbinger

This is a good tall outdoor cordon variety which can also be grown in a tunnel or cold glasshouse. Fruit have a wonderful flavour; they are thin-skinned and medium sized, and will ripen well off the plant.

Long-Keeping

This tomato is large, round and very well-flavoured, but incredibly slow to ripen on the vine unless grown in hot sun. Relatively acid, fruits will continue to ripen slowly in storage, and they keep for months.

Principe Borghese

A traditional Italian tomato for preserving. Bushy plants produce fruits which are very dense with few seeds and little juice, perfect for drying in the sun, when they become quite delicious.

Costoluto Genovese

This bushy old Italian variety prefers full sun to produce bright red flattened globe-shaped fruits, soft in texture, very juicy and slightly tart – perfect for juicing. They keep better than many soft-fruited varieties.

Merveille des Marchés

Productive and vigorous plants are bushy and compact, producing large red fruits with pink flesh. They are well adapted to most climates, reliable and tasty.

St Pierre

This old variety is one of the favourites of French traditional gardeners. Midseason tall strong plants produce large fruits of very good quality and taste.

Abraham Lincoln

Introduced at the beginning of the 20th century, red medium-sized fruits are uniform and free of defects. The bronze-green foliage is disease resistant, and tomatoes have a distinctive slightly acidic flavour which appeals to many. This cordon growing variety will flourish even in rainy and cooler summers.

Marmande

Very popular in France, vigorous bushy plants should be staked to produce masses of slightly irregular-shaped red beefsteak fruits with firm flesh and excellent flavour late in the season. This variety will fruit reliably and productively even in low temperatures.

Red Peach

This variety produces very small tasty fruits with a slightly fuzzy peach-like skin. The flavour is very good but, unlike another peach-skinned variety, **Garden Peach,** these do not store well and are best eaten straight off the vine.

Bosnian Beefsteak

This enormous beefsteak tomato can be found under various names in Southeastern Europe. It seems to have been selected to flourish in drought. Leaves are small and hang limp during heat waves, but the fruits are large and juicy, typically weighing around 1kg (2lb), with few seeds and distinctive flavour. Leave sideshoots unless the growth becomes restricted. The large size and thin skins of the fruits mean that they can tend to crack in prolonged dry periods.

Stupice

Potato leaf variety that originated in Czechoslovakia but became popular in the US, taken there 25 years ago. It is very early and reliable, and extremely productive with very tasty fruits. It can grow well over 1m (6ft) tall, and thrives in cool climates.

OTHER COLOURS

Brandywine

This is an Amish family heirloom from the US, dating back to at least 1885. Preserved by pioneer grower Ben Quisenbury, from New England, who maintained hundreds of varieties of tomatoes during his life. When he died aged 95 he passed his legacy to the Seed Savers Exchange in Iowa, from where this variety has spread and spread. Reddish-pink, very large thin-skinned fruits, sometimes with dark patches, are borne on potato-leaf vines. Although the tall vines are not disease resistant the tomatoes are quite delicious, best in salads and sandwiches.

Potato-Leaf White

A cordon variety, with characteristic potato leaves and large beefy tomatoes that ripen to an attractive pale cream colour. It is the most reliable of the white tomatoes, with thin skin and excellent flavour. Sadly, it has very few seeds, so will never be very common.

Golden Sunrise

Listed in European catalogues in the 1890s, this cordon tomato produces medium-sized golden yellow, fruits which are round and thin-skinned. Early and heavy cropping, their flavour is superb.

Garden Peach

Cordon-type plants produce small orange-pink fruit with slightly fuzzy peach-like skin blushed with pink. Prolific, soft-skinned and juicy when ripe, the flavour is good but the outstanding thing about this tomato is its keeping quality. It is best grown in a glasshouse or polytunnel in cooler areas, as this variety is slow to crop, but even if fruits don't ripen fully you can bring them inside and store them for several months, and they will slowly continue to ripen without going soft or losing flavour.

Russian

Dark coloured thin-skinned fruits are incredibly juicy, and the cordon-type plants grow well under most conditions. The taste is enhanced with a slightly smoky saltiness – ideal for salads. Fruits do not store well, but you will probably want to eat them straight away. The colour and flavour are best when grown in full sun and reasonable heat, so these are best grown under cover in much of Northern Europe for eating off the vine, but unripe ones make wonderful preserves.

Bitchyeh Gertzeh / Bull's Heart

This very old Russian variety is traditionally grown for bragging purposes, and to separate the amateurs from the experts! Plants can grow to 2m (6ft) tall, and large pink oxheart shaped fruits average 10cm (4in), but have been known to grow to 1.8kg (4lb). This is difficult to grow, but definitely worth a try if you are feeling adventurous!

Hugh's

This pale yellow beefsteak variety is a reliably productive North American heirloom. It develops a delicious flavour, particularly in sunny conditions, but is most prized for its thirst-quenching qualities, as it is extremely large and juicy,

Mr Stripey / Tigerella

This unusual English heirloom is highly productive, producing small yellow fleshed fruits with numerous pink stripes and a pink heart on bushy plants. Flavour is mild, and small fruits are low in acid.

Golden Queen

This is one of the oldest yellow tomatoes still available, originally popular in Europe in the 1880s. Bushy plants produce exceptionally sweet good sized round yellow-orange fruits.

Persimmon

The huge rich orange-gold coloured fruits of this historic variety weigh up to 1kg (2lb). The flesh is very firm, with few seeds, and a unique flavour. Although the tall vigorous plants are not as productive as some modern varieties, they grow reliably in most circumstances and are definitely worth trying for their striking appearance and taste.

Arkansas Traveller

Another very old variety, the tall plants grow best in hot and humid areas, and are resistant to most pests and diseases. The fruits are flattened pink globes, without any tendency to split.

Pineapple / Ananas

This old potato leaf cordon variety produces huge and attractive fruits with distinctive yellow skins with red patches. The flesh is very firm, yellow striped with red, and it looks rather similar to pineapple flesh.

Tomatillos

Large Green

Grow this variety like an outdoor tomato; it has purple-blotched yellow flowers followed by green fruits enclosed in a papery husk. Ripe fruits are quite sweet and can be eaten as snacks or in salads, and unripe fruits are used in a wide variety of Mexican dishes such as salsa verde.

Purple

This variety has smaller fruit with a sharper flavour, and is preferred by some Mexican cooks.

TURNIPS
Brassica rapa (Cruciferae)

It is believed that turnips were cultivated in Europe in prehistoric times. They were definitely popular with the Romans and many other early cultures in Europe and Asia, and a great diversity of forms developed.

In 1885 Vilmorin listed well over 50 varieties in *The Vegetable Garden*, including those with yellow, white, black, purple and red-tinted skins, and round, flat or long tapering roots. Very few of these are still around today, but it is worth keeping an eye out for traditional varieties.

The roots of large winter turnips are usually used in soups and stews, while young fresh summer turnips are more tender and more versatile. In Japan they are traditionally used raw and pickled as well as cooked.

Turnips thrive in cool moist conditions, in soil containing plenty of organic matter. Sow quick-maturing summer types from early spring, they are unlikely to succeed in hot dry weather. Winter types are normally sown in late summer, and can be left in the ground until severe frosts set in.

Turnips are biennial, forming flower stalks in their second year. Their flowers are insect pollinated, and crossing will occur with other turnips and with some Oriental greens and fodder crops.

Black Sugarsweet
A long-rooted turnip with very sweet firm white flesh. Plants have an abundance of dark green split leaves, and are quick to mature. The roots keep well in winter.

Gammal Svensk
One of a number of old local Scandinavian varieties still in cultivation, this variety has large elongated roots and yellow flesh. It has a very strong flavour.

Laird's Victory / Sharpes Eclipse
An old English long-rooted variety developed by the Lincolnshire firm of Sharpe and Co, and exhibited by the Scottish seed merchant Laird & Sinclair at their centenary in 1933.

Golden Ball
This tastes more like a swede than a turnip and has been grown since the 1850s. Yellow globes are around 10cm (4 in) diameter with sweet golden flesh, ideal for mashing. Use as a summer turnip or for store it for winter storage.

Rave d'Auvergne Hâtive / Early Flat Redtop Auvergne
The name sums it up – it is early, with a very flat top of which the above-ground portion is violet-red. Very productive, with tall abundant leaves, this tasty variety needs plenty of space.

Veitch's Red Globe

Fast maturing, smooth-skinned roots have red tops and pure white flesh with a very good flavour. Good for short season areas, this variety stores well.

Petrowski

This very old variety is a gourmet specialty from Berlin. Round yellow roots have white flesh which is firm and sweet with an aromatic after taste. This probably has the most delicate taste of all turnips, and definitely merits a place in any garden.

WATERMELONS
Citrullus lanatus *(Cucurbitaceae)*

Watermelons come from tropical Africa where they have been in cultivation for thousands of years, but some of the most interesting landraces are found in Central Asia. Botanists first recorded watermelons in Europe in the 13th century.

They need a long hot growing season and although they are traditionally grown in Mediterranean areas they have rarely been considered worth cultivating in Northern Europe. However, there are a few cool climate varieties that could be grown with the protection of a glasshouse or polytunnel.

Watermelons need a reasonably fertile moisture retentive soil and plenty of water throughout the growing season. Flowers are normally insect–pollinated, and crossing will occur with other watermelons although not with melons.

Cream of Saskatchewan

This very old-fashioned variety is perfectly adapted to cooler climates. Large round green-skinned fruits have cream to pale yellow flesh. The flavour is very sweet and delicious. One word of warning – these fruits tend to explode at the slightest bump, so you are unlikely ever to find them sold in shops or markets!

Sugarbaby

This variety is comparatively recent, introduced about 50 years ago, but worth growing as an early crop in a polytunnel or glasshouse. Ideal where space is limited, numerous small round fruits are produced on very compact vines; the rind of these sweet, red-fleshed fruits turns greenish black when ripe.

THE DIRECTORY – RESOURCES
SEED SUPPLIERS

While we have done our best to ensure that this information is accurate and up-to-date at the time of publication, companies do change hands or take a break, and new ones start trading. No list such as this can ever be comprehensive, and there are sure to be some we have not included. We apologise for any omissions or inaccuracies, and thank all suppliers for providing a wonderful service in saving and supplying seeds for the future. Any prices quoted are correct at the time of printing.

UNITED KINGDOM

Jennifer Birch
Garfield Villa
Bellevue Road,
Stroud,
Gloucestershire GL5 2BS
Tel: 01453 750371

Supplier of named varieties of French seed garlic, certified as pest and disease free. Traditional and new varieties.
● Catalogue: send postage

Chilterns Seeds
Bortree Stile
Ulverston, Cumbria
LA12 7PB
Tel: 01229 581137
Fax: 01229 584549
e-mail: 101 344.1340@compuserve.com

Supply many seeds that are not easy to get elsewhere; although most are ornamental and wild plants, they have a small range of vegetables including some unusual varieties and Oriental vegetables.

Thomas Etty Esq
45 Forde Avenue
Bromley,
Kent BR1 3EU
Tel:0181 466 6785
e-mail: rwarner@cix.compulink.co.uk

Catalogue of traditional British vegetable varieties, nearly all of which were introduced before 1900. The catalogue entries include quotes from gardening journals of the time. Etty also sells herb seeds.
● Catalogue: £1.00

Mr Fothergill's Seeds
Gazeley Road,
Kentford,
Newmarket,
Suffolk CB8 7QB
Tel: 01638 751161
Fax: 01638 751624

Large seed company which markets a range of vegetables, herbs and flowers. They have recently introduced some heritage seeds, together with plants of varieties not on the EC list.
● Catalogue: free within the UK.

Future Foods
PO Box 1564
Wedmore,
Somerset BS28 4DP
Tel: 01934 713602
Fax: 01934 713623
e-mail: ff@seeds.compulink.co.uk

Small independent seed company selling 'weird and wonderful things for the edible garden'. Their catalogue contains many unusual salads, roots, tubers and other vegetables, including some old varieties not found in other commercial catalogues.
● Catalogue: £1.00 or 4 first class stamps within the UK.

M & A Innes
Old Town,
Brownhill,
Newmacher,
Aberdeen AB21 7PR
Tel: 01651 862333

The Inneses took over the famous Maclean potato collection. They maintain over 400 varieties, and their catalogue of potatoes offers a selection of these each year.

E W King
Coggeshall Road,
Kelvedon,
Essex CO5 9PG
Tel: 01376 570000
Fax: 01376 571189

Large well established independent seed company, supplying a wide range of modern and traditional vegetable varieties, herbs and flowers. Kings' have been responsible for saving several old varieties about to be dropped from the National List.

Chase Organics
The Organic Gardening Catalogue
Coombelands House,
Addlestone,
Surrey KT15 1HY
Tel: 01932 820958
Fax: 01932 829322

A mail order catalogue run jointly by Chase Organics and the **Henry Doubleday Research Association** (*see page 176*). Supplies a large range of vegetable seeds including a good proportion of traditional varieties and a special 19th century vegetable collection. Also green manure, flower, and herb seeds and books.
● Catalogue: free within the UK.

Alan Romans' Potato Seed Varieties
Marketed through the
Organic Gardening Catalogue (*see above*)

Alan Romans is a potato specialist, and this catalogue makes over 200 potato varieties available to gardeners. It gives the date of introduction and origin for each variety, as well as detailed cultural characteristics and expert comments.
● Catalogue: £1.00.

Seeds-by-Size
45 Crouchfield
Boxmoor,
Hemel Hempstead,
Hertfordshire HP1 1PA
Tel: 01442 251458
e-mail: John-Robert-Size @ Seeds-by-Size.Co.UK

This extensive seed list includes a very large range of open-pollinated vegetable varieties (eg 24 parsnips, over 50 lettuce). Seeds are sold by weight. They have a separate list of F1 hybrids.
● Catalogue: send large SAE.

Simpson's Seeds
27 Meadowbrook,
Old Oxted,
Surrey RH8 9LT
Tel/Fax: 01883 715242

Simpsons describe themselves as a 'kitchen table' business, a small family-run seed firm. They supply modern and traditional vegetable varieties, with a particularly wide range of peppers and tomatoes. They also sell the plants of some varieties which are not on the National List.

Suffolk Herbs
Monks Farm
Coggeshall Road,
Kelvedon, Essex
CO5 9PG
Tel: 01376 572456
Fax: 01376 571189

Suffolk Herbs have a reputation for a comprehensive list of vegetable seeds, with the emphasis on traditional and unusual varieties. They also offer a good range of Oriental vegetables, and supply green manure, herb and flower seeds, and books. Part of **E W King** seeds (*see separate entry*).
● Catalogue: free within the UK.

Thompson & Morgan
Poplar Lane,
Ipswich,
Suffolk IP8 3BU
Tel: 01473 688588
Fax: 01473 680199

Large UK-based seed company, also operating in France
and Germany, and in the US. They offer a relatively small
range of vegetables compared to an enormous range of
flowers, and many are modern hybrids, but their
catalogue always contains some unusual crops. They also
offer some new introductions of particular interest to
amateur gardeners (see page 68).
● Catalogue: free within UK, France, Germany.

Edwin Tucker & Sons Ltd
Brewery Meadow,
Stonepark,
Ashburton,
Devon TQ13 7DG
Tel: 01364 652403
Fax: 01364 654300

Well established West Country seed company supplying a
range of traditional and modern vegetables and flowers.
They still maintain one or two traditional local varieties
that they bred.

Websters Seed Potatoes
Unit 16
Ogilvy Place,
Arbroath,
Tayside DD11 4DE
Tel: 01241 673473

A potato specialist, offering over 100 varieties in 1997,
including a few that are unlikely to be found in many
other catalogues.

DENMARK

Froposen
Karlebovej 24,
2980 Kokkedal
Tel: 42 18 03 12

A small independent seed company selling a limited range
of mainly traditional vegetable varieties; also herbs,
flowers, books.

FRANCE

B&T World Seeds
Route des Marchandes,
Paguigan,
34210 Olonzac
Tel: 04 68 91 29 63
Fax: 04 68 91 30 39
e-mail: R@thesys.demon.co.uk

This company's Master Seed List contains around 35,000
entries of seeds from around the world, including native
species, cultivated plants and vegetable varieties, but
without descriptions or cultural information. Thematic
sub-lists are available (or can be compiled) which give
some details to help you find the plants you are interested
in. Most entries are supplied as seeds, but a few as bulbs
or plants. The lists are available printed or on disk.
● Master list: £10 printed post paid in Europe, £5 on disk.

Biau Germe
47360 Montpezat
Tel/Fax: 05 53 95 95 04

A cooperatively run seed company which has 7 hectares
of land growing organic and biodynamic seeds for
gardeners and small growers. They specialise particularly
in traditional and regionally adapted French varieties, and
they have campaigned vigorously against the legislation
that makes it illegal for them to sell some of these. As
well as a range of open-pollinated vegetables, the catalogue contains green manure seeds, some herbs and
flowers.
● Catalogue: 20F.

Ferme de Sainte Marthe
BP10,
41700 Cour Cheverny
Tel: 02 54 44 20 86
Fax: 02 54 44 21 70

This catalogue has seeds of old and unusual vegetable
varieties – all open-pollinated. Old varieties are clearly
marked and there are good colour photographs of many.
The seeds produced at la Ferme de Sainte Marthe are
organically grown, although others in the catalogue may
not be (again clearly marked). Relevant books and videos
are also listed. Ferme de Ste Martha also supply green
manure seeds, fruit, old fashioned flowers and roses. They
have a shop at Millancay.
● Catalogue: 20F.

Germinance
Les Rétifs,
49150 St Martin D'Arcé
Tel / fax: 02 41 82 73 23

This catalogue offers biodynamically produced open-pollinated vegetable varieties for gardeners and small growers, and includes many old and traditional varieties, also some herbs and flowers. This is another company that has made a stand against the seed legislation.
● Catalogue: large SAE or postal coupons outside France (donations welcome).

Graines Baumaux
BP100
54062 Nancy Cedex
Tel: 03 83 15 86 86
Fax: 03 83 15 86 80

A large commercial seed company whose well illustrated catalogue has a very wide range of vegetables including many old and unusual varieties, as well as modern hybrids.
● Catalogue: 24F.

Terre de Semence
BP 2
03210 St-Menoux
Tel: 04 70 43 96 92
Fax: 04 70 43 96 83

One of the main stated aims of Terre de Semence is to promote the protection of biodiversity by making seeds of endangered varieties widely available to gardeners, and also by giving support to relevant projects in developing countries. Their catalogue contains a whole range of old and unusual open-pollinated vegetable varieties, particularly peppers, tomatoes and squashes. Old varieties are clearly marked. Seeds of herbs, grains and flowers are also supplied. All seeds are organically or biodynamically grown. The catalogue includes articles on the history and cultivation of some of the crops, and on issues concerning biodiversity.
● Catalogue: 40F.

Vilmorin
BP 37
38291 St-Quentin F. Cedex
Tel: 04 74 82 11 11

The famous French seed firm started by the Vilmorin family 250 years ago, sells a few traditional varieties along with modern introductions.
● Catalogue: 20F.

GERMANY

Allerleirauh GmbH
Saatguthandel,
Kronstrasse 24
61209 Echzell

This company offers a range of open-pollinated vegetables, biodynamically produced, including a number of traditional varieties. Also herb and flower seeds.
● Catalogue: DM5 within Germany, DM10 to other European countries.

Dreschflegel
Föckinghauser Weg 9,
49324 Melle
Tel: 05422 8994

A small supplier offering a range of open-pollinated vegetables, including some old and unusual varieties, biodynamically produced. Also herb and flower seeds.
● Catalogue: SAE within Germany, send postal coupons if requesting catalogue from outside Germany.

Monika Gehlsen
Willi Dolgner Strasse 17,
06118 Halle
Tel: 0345 522 64 23

This catalogue offers seeds of many less common plants, both edible and ornamental. Includes a small but expanding range of old and unusual vegetables.

Kräuterzauber
Am Himpberg 32,
27367 Stuckenborstel
Tel: 04264 2284
Fax: 04264 2230

A comprehensive catalogue of herbs, with some salads and unusual edible plants. Both seeds and plants are supplied.
● Catalogue: DM5 within Germany, DM10 to other European countries.

Küchengarten
Postfach 1511,
73505 Schwäbisch Gmünd
tel: 07171 928712
Fax: 07171 39843

A good range of open-pollinated vegetable varieties,
emphasising traditional varieties from around Europe,
and also a selection of Oriental vegetables, herbs and a
few flowers.
● Catalogue: free in Germany, £5.00 for UK customers.

THE NETHERLANDS

Vitalis Biologishe Zaden
Hengelderweg 6,
7383 RG, Voorst
Tel: 0575 502648
Fax: 0575 502987

A small biodynamic seed company producing seed of
both old and new open-pollinated vegetable varieties.
They select varieties suitable for organic and biodynamic
growing, and also carry out some plant breeding, experi-
menting with a wide range of varieties from sources
around the world.

De Bolster
P. Venemakade 61,
9605PL Kielwindeweer
Tel: 31 598 491534
Fax: 31 598 491623

A small company producing a range of biodynamically
grown vegetables and flower seeds for home gardeners.

SWEDEN

Bernhard Anderssons Fröhandel
38522 Torsås

Long-established small seed company, still selling some
old varieties.

Runåbergs Fröer
Känstorp 7368
44493 Spekeröd

Small seed company aiming to supply old varieties.

Svalöff-Weibulls
26800 Svalöff

Large well established seed company, still selling some
traditional Swedish-bred varieties.

SWITZERLAND

Gärtnerei am Ekkharthof
8574 Lengwil
Tel: 071 686 6655
Fax: 071 686 6656

A small well established company producing biodynamically grown seeds. They supply a good range of
open-pollinated vegetables, some old, some more recent,
and also carry out plant breeding. Sales of seed in
Switzerland are not bound by EC regulations.

C and R Zollinger
Biologische Samen,
1891 Les Evouette
Tel: 025 81 40 35

Christine and Robert Zollinger produce seeds biodynamically on 7 hectares of land at Les Evouette. They collect
and maintain many old types and varieties which are not
on the EC list. Their catalogue contains a wonderful range
of vegetables – some common, some rare – plus herbs
and flowers, and is being extended annually
● Catalogue: large SAE or postal coupon if requesting
catalogue from outside Switzerland.

UNITED STATES

Abundant Life Seed Foundation
PO Box 772,
Port Townsend, WA 98368
Tel: 360 385 5660
Fax: 360 385 7455

Non-profit corporation which aims to preserve genetic
diversity and support sustainable agriculture through
acquiring, propagating, and preserving native and natu-
ralised seed, with specific emphasis on those species not
commercially available, including rare and endangered
species. They established the World Seed Fund in 1985 to
send seeds to impoverished communities worldwide.

All seeds are open-pollinated, many are organically
grown or wildcrafted.
● Catalogue: $2.00 + Large SAE or postal coupon.

Bountiful Gardens
18001 Shafer Ranch Road,
Willits, CA 95490
Tel/fax: 707 459 6410
website: http://www.olympus.net/gardens/welcome.html

Specialising in heirloom varieties, Bountiful Gardens is a family-run organisation supplying over 300 varieties of open-pollinated untreated seeds, organically, bio-intensively or naturally grown. They also supply a range of **seeds from the HDRA in the UK.**
● Ships seeds abroad.
● Heirloom catalogue free with SAE.
● Rare seeds catalogue $2.00 + SAE.
● Bulk pricelist $1.00 + SAE.

Fish Lake Garlic Man
Ted Mackza
Research and Experimental Station
RR2, Demorestville
Ontario
KOK 1WO
Tel: 613 476 8030

A non-profit organisation, dedicated to 'making Canada self-sufficient in garlic, and to developing the finest garlic in the world'! A wide variety of garlics, plus useful cultivation information.
● Price list and information $3.00 + postal coupon.

High Altitude Gardens
PO Box 1048
Hailey
ID 83333-1048
Tel: *catalog requests* 208 788 4363
queries and orders 208 788 4419
Fax: 208 788 3452
e-mail: higarden@micron.net
Website:http://trine.com/Garden
Net/higarden.htm

Family-run bioregional seed company, growing open-pollinated seeds adapted to cold short seasons, all tested at 6,000 feet – most do very well at low altitudes too. Dedicated to sustainable agriculture, their **Seeds Trust** encourages and teaches seed saving. As well as a wide variety of vegetables, High Altitude Gardens also sell elusive wildflowers and native grasses.
● Ships seed worldwide.
● Catalogues include classics and heirlooms lists – send large SAE.

Seeds of Change
PO Box 15700,
Santa Fe, NM 87506-5700
Tel: 505 438 8080
Fax: 505 438 7052
e-mail: gardener@seeds of change.com
Website: www.seeds of change.com

Over 400 varieties of open-pollinated seed for vegetables, flowers, and herbs, including many heirloom varieties, produced organically. Aims to further awareness of sustainable agriculture techniques and socially responsible food production.
● Ships seed worldwide.
● Catalog $1.00 + SAE or postal coupon.

ORGANISATIONS INVOLVED WITH GENETIC CONSERVATION

UNITED KINGDOM

Heritage Seed Library
Henry Doubleday Research Association (HDRA)
Ryton Organic Gardens
Ryton-on-Dunsmore,
Coventry CV8 3LG
Tel: 01203 303517
Fax: 01203 639229
e-mail: enquiry@hdra.org.uk

The Henry Doubleday Research Association established its Seed Library in 1975 as a response to the threat to vegetable varieties posed by European legislation. It currently contains around 600 varieties. Stocks are maintained both at HDRA and by Seed Guardians around the country who are each responsible for one or more varieties. HDRA also have a potato collection of old varieties, initially obtained from virus-free stock at the Commonwealth Potato Collection in Edinburgh, and now maintained as microplants. At present these are multiplied up into 'mini-tubers' in aphid-proof tunnels at HDRA before they are distributed. They also have a tuber collection awaiting a virus eradication programme.

Each year members of the Heritage Seed Library receive three newsletters, and a catalogue containing a selection of Seed Library varieties from which they can obtain free seeds. The catalogue also contains a Seed Swap Register, enabling members to exchange seeds.

HDRA campaign nationally and in Europe on issues concerning genetic diversity. Their publications include the *Fruit and Vegetable Finder* which lists legally available varieties and their sources, enabling the many open-pollinated vegetables available from just one or two suppliers to be pin-pointed and promoted.

Some of the Seed Library varieties can be seen growing at HDRA's two demonstration gardens: Ryton Organic Gardens near Coventry and Yalding Organic Gardens in Kent. Events such as Potato Day (*see page 89*) are also held there. There are a number of other gardens open to the public where vegetables from HDRA's Seed Library can be seen growing:

Ripley Castle Gardens
Ripley Castle Estate Office,
Ripley,
Nr Harrogate,
North Yorks HG3 3AY
Tel: 01423 770152
Many acres of gardens and parkland, and a 5 acre Victorian walled garden.

Sudeley Castle and Gardens
Sudeley Castle,
Winchcombe,
Gloucestershire GL54 5JD
Tel: 01242 602308
Recently restored vegetable garden of medieval Cotswold Castle.

Drenewydd Museum
26-27 Lower Row,
Bute Town,
Rhymney NP22 5QH
Tel: 01685 843039
A recreation of household life in the heyday of the iron-working industry at the end of the 19th century; includes a period garden.

Quarry Bank Mill
Styal,
Wilmslow,
Cheshire SK9 4LA
Tel: 01625 527468
A working museum of the cotton industry, which includes a late 18th century Apprentice House Garden, where young apprentices to the Mill would have grown their own crops.

West Dean Gardens
Estate Office,
The Edward James Foundation,
West Dean,
Chichester,
West Sussex PO18 0QZ
Tel: 01243 818210
The many acres of grounds at West Dean include a $2^{1}/_{2}$ acre walled kitchen garden, recreated as it would have been in Edwardian times (*see page 78*).

Normanby Hall Country Park
Normanby,
Scunthorpe,
North Lincolnshire DN15 9HU
Tel: 01724 720588
Normanby Hall has parkland, woodland and formal gardens, including a Victorian walled kitchen garden growing 19th century vegetables, flowers and fruit.

Hercules Garden
Hercules Garden House,
Blair Atholl,
Pitlochry,
Perthshire PH18 5TX
The Hercules garden, which dates back to 1744, is in the grounds of Blair Castle and has recently been extensively restored.

The SAFE Alliance
38 Ebury Street,
London SW1W 0LU
Tel: 0171 823 5660
Fax: 0171 823 5673
e-mail: safe@gn.apc.org

The SAFE Alliance (Sustainable Agriculture, Food and Environment) links a range of farmer, consumer and environmental organisations in the UK and Europe, with the aim of promoting a sustainable system of food production and marketing. They work through lobbying and campaigning, organising meetings and conferences, and have researched and published several reports on biodiversity in food and farming.

Intermediate Technology Development Group (ITDG)
Myson House,
Railway Terrace,
Rugby CV21 3HT
Tel: 01788 560631
Fax: 01788 540270
e-mail: enquiries@itdg.org.uk.

ITDG have a 'food security' programme, working directly with communities in the South. Its aim is to allow such communities to sustain their traditional role of developing diversity in their crops and livestock. Several reports and booklets on this work have been published.
    ITDG have recently initiated the formation of the UK Agricultural Biodiversity Coalition (UKABC), an alliance of public interest groups concerned with agricultural biodiversity. It provides information, develops projects and programmes, carries out research, and lobbies the institutions that govern agricultural biodiversity both nationally and internationally.

AUSTRIA

Arche Noah
Ober Strasse 40,
3553 Schloss Schiltern
Tel: 02734 8626
Fax: 02734 8627

Arche Noah was established as a seed saving network in the early 1990s, mainly as a response to the decline in local plant breeding and seed production, and the consequent disappearance of many regionally adapted varieties. It now has around 2500 members. and maintains over 3500 plant varieties, a good proportion of which are vegetables. About 1000 varieties are grown out every year and can be seen in the 'preservation gardens', a historic baroque garden, open to the public on Saturday afternoons in summer.
    Arche Noah produce a yearly catalogue offering seed, and members also receive a newsletter. In the last few years Arche Noah has cooperated with the Seed Savers Exchange in the US in arranging seed collecting missions in Eastern Europe and the Mediterranean.

CANADA

Seeds of Diversity Canada
Formerly **Heritage Seed Program**
Box 36,
Station Q,
Toronto ONM4T 2L7

Membership scheme and seed exchange programmes, founded by the Canadian Organic Growers in 1984, dedicated to preserving heirloom and endangered flowers, vegetables, herbs and grains. Members receive a quarterly magazine and annual seed listing.
Overseas Membership: $30.00.

DENMARK

Center vor Bio-diversitet
Hvejselvej 127,
7300 Jelling

The objective of the Center is to support biological diversity in both crops and domestic animals. Some traditional local crop varieties have been rediscovered and evaluated, and the Center aims to spread interest in such varieties to ensure their survival.

EIRE

Irish Seed Savers Association
Capparoe,
Scariff,
Co Clare

This seedsavers network maintains a collection of non-commercially available vegetable varieties, and aims to seek out and reintroduce traditional Irish varieties of fruit and vegetables. A selection of seeds is offered to members in an annual listing, and in turn members are asked to return some saved seed to the Association. There is also a seed-swap register. The group have recently set up a Heritage Garden at Scariff.

FINLAND

SESAM
PO Box 140
00251 Helsingore
Tel: 358 9 70300721
Fax: 358 9 70300791

This sister organisation to SESAM in Sweden has a membhership of about 200 – both amateur gardeners and experts – and is closely connected to Finland's research institutions and the Nordic Gene Bank. SESAM Finland also has connections with a small company (translates as **Grandmother's Plants**) which sells seeds and plants of old varieties including Finnish and Estonian types of swedes, turnips, onions and garlic, and over 100 different potatoes.

FRANCE

Ecomusée de la Corneuve
38 Avenue de la Republique,
93120 La Corneuve
Tel: 02 48 38 31 18

The Ecomusée researches and organises exhibits on the history of fruit and vegetable production, focusing on the region around Paris. Its main aim is to encourage the popularity of traditional varieties and hence keep them in commercial production. Twice a year they hold a 'Marché au Musée', selling locally grown produce (*see page 173*).

The Musée de Culture Légumières at Corneuve presents the daily life of market gardeners in the region at the turn of the century, and some of the vegetable varieties of that time are grown in the gardens.

Plantes et Fruits Brayons
15 Place Maintenon,
76680 Saint-Saëns
Tel: 02 35 34 51 35

A local organisation formed with the aim of seeking out and protecting plants and animals traditional to the region, and also preserving the associated methods of cultivation and husbandry. They offer advice to farmers and growers, and stage exhibitions and fairs and other promotional events. A number of old vegetable varieties have been rediscovered and brought back into use.

Terre Vivante
Domaine de Raud,
BP 20,
38711 Mens
Tel: 04 76 34 80 80
Fax: 04 76 34 84 02

Terre Vivante have an Ecological Centre in the foothills of the Isère in South East France. They have a commitment to genetic conservation, and many traditional varieties can be seen growing in the demonstration gardens at the Centre. Events and courses, such as one-day workshops on old potato varieties, are also held there.

Terre Vivante publish an organic gardening magazine and books on ecological topics, and at present are helping compile a catalogue of endangered vegetable varieties — ones that do not appear in the commercial French and European catalogues; this is due for publication in 1998.

Club Memoire Verte
BP20,
33670 La Sauve Majeure

An association established in the mid 1980s to research into and save old local vegetable varieties. The association runs a seed saving network.

Centre Régional de Resources Génétiques
Ferme du Héron,
Chemin de la Ferme Lenglet,
59650 Villeneuve-d'Ascq
Tel: 20 67 03 51
Fax: 20 67 03 37

A local organisation aiming to seek out and reintroduce traditional fruit and vegetable varieties of the Nord-Pas-de-Calais region. This was once a large thriving market gardening area where many local varieties were developed, and a number have recently been rediscovered. Ferme du Héron has gardens and an orchard, and there is a network of farmers and gardeners growing the traditional varieties and saving seed.

GERMANY

Pflanzenzucht Wernstein
Wernstein 24
95336 Mainleus
Tel: 09229 8157

Pflanzenzucht Wernstein is a well established biodynamic research association. They maintain a large collection of old local varieties of vegetables and field crops (50 varieties of garlic and 60 varieties of potatoes, for example), which are used in developing cultivation systems and breeding varieties for biodynamic production. They do not generally make seeds available, but arrange meetings, tours of their gardens and other events.

THE NETHERLANDS

Stichting het Hof van Eden
PO Box 636
3500 AP Utrecht
Tel: 31 30 2516941

Started by Guus Lieberworth in 1979, the **Court of Eden** has become Europe's largest private collection of plant genetic resources. It maintains more than 30,000 samples of seed from all over the world – many from minor crops and old varieties – and has exchanged seeds with gene banks and research institutes in various countries. The Court of Eden has a garden, recently relocated, but many of the seeds in the collection are grown out on small plots around Utrecht.

De Kleine Aarde
Postbus 151,
5280 AD Boxtel
Tel: 0411 68 49 21
Fax: 0411 68 34 07

An environmental organisation with a commitment to promoting ecological farming and growing, including the use of appropriate local varieties. They have demonstration gardens at Boxtel.

St Museum 'De Oerakker'
8433 MN Haulerwijk
Tel: 31 516 422933

This organisation conserves old varieties of vegetables and field crops.

SWEDEN

SESAM
Snödroppsvägen 12,
146 50 Tullinge
Tel: 08 778 48 51
Fax: 08 608 21 77

SESAM is a seedsaving network with around 250 members. It is a voluntary organisation but has close relations with the Nordic gene bank. The group's primary concern is seeking out and maintaining original Nordic varieties of vegetables and field crops, and its members have found and rescued many local landraces and old commercial varieties. Peas, beans, turnips and potatoes, are amongst the crops particularly well represented. The group also maintains varieties from other countries with a long tradition of cultivation in Sweden.

The members of SESAM grow the crops and save seed, which is offered in an annual 'Yearbook'; samples are also kept in cold storage in a central seed bank. SESAM has a sister organisation in Finland.

SWITZERLAND

Pro Specie Rara
Engelgasse 12a
9000 St Gallen
Tel: 071 222 74 20
Fax: 071 223 74 01

A private organisation established in the early 1980s with the aim of conserving old breeds of animals and old fruit, vegetable and cereal varieties, and bringing them back into use. The crops they are particularly concerned with are those that are adapted to the high altitude and harsh conditions of the Swiss mountain climate.

A network of growers maintain the varieties that Pro Specie Rara have collected, and return to them a proportion of their seed together with notes on their experiences with the crops. The organisation also runs courses and other events.

UNITED STATES

Seed Savers Exchange
3076 North Winn Road
Decorah
IA 52101
Tel: (319) 382-5990
Fax: (319) 382-5872

The initial and principal seed saving network in the US, SSE has an extensive seed bank and a 170 acre farm, open to visitors, where heirloom varieties are grown out. At the Heritage Farm, permanent collections are maintained and displayedin 9 large organic Preservation Gardens and a Historic Orchard containing 700 19th century apples and 200 hardy grapes. They also keep herds of Ancient White Park cattle.

The collection of seeds at Heritage Farm recently exceeded 18,000 varieties: 4,100 tomatoes, 3,600 beans, 1,200 peppers, 1,000 squash, 900 peas, 800 lettuces, 600 corns, 400 melons, 200 watermelons and 200 garlics. Every year the seeds of about 2,000 varieties are multiplied in the Preservation Gardens, processed and heat-sealed into foil packets, stored in the basement of the office complex. Excess seeds (beyond our grow-out needs) are then made available to SSE's members.

Seed Savers Membership include an annual copy of the *Seed Savers Yearbook*,with the addresses of more than 1,000 members, and 12,000 listings of rare and unusual vegetable seeds.
Overseas Membership: US $40.00.

Seed Savers International (SSI)
Seed Savers Exchange (*see previous entry*)

SSI is a project organised by SSE supporting a network of plant collectors in genetically rich Eastern European countries who are rescuing traditional food crops that are in danger of extinction. SSI has established working relationships with scientists at the Gaterslaben seed bank in Eastern Germany, and the Vavilov Institute in St Petersburg. Half of the seeds collected by SSI are donated to the host country's seed bank; the other half is taken back to Gaterslaben or the Vavilov Institute, where scientists split the samples again and send a portion to Heritage Farm. Since 1993, seeds of 3,000 traditional vegetable varieties from 30 Eastern countries have been collected and saved.

Native Seeds/SEARCH
2509 N Campbell Ave #325
Tucson
AZ 85719
Tel: 520 327 9123
Fax: 520 327 5821

A non-profit group working to conserve traditional crops, seeds, and farming methods of the US Southwest and Northern Mexico. Native Seeds/SEARCH promotes the use of native plants and their wild relatives and works to preserve knowledge about their uses through research, training, and community education. Native Seeds/SEARCH has a demonstration garden in the grounds of the Tucson Botanical Gardens.

Members receive 10% discount on all purchases and workshops, and quarterly newsletter The Seedhead News. Dedicated to the preservation of endangered native plants, and to redistributing native crops, NSS hold various events at their trial gardens throughout the year.
Overseas Membership: $40.00.

ECHO Seed Sales
17430 Durrance Road
North Fort Myers
FL 33917-2239
Tel: (941) 543-3246
Fax: (941) 543-5317
email: echo@xc.org
Website: www.xc.org/echo

ECHO (Educational Concerns for Hunger Organization) is a non-profit Christian organisation with a seed bank for under utilized tropical plants. Seeds are supplied free to overseas development workers. Small amounts of seed sold to others.
All seeds are treated with insecticide and fungicide, only suitable for subtropical regions.

FURTHER READING

Finding Heritage Vegetables

The Fruit and Vegetable Finder
ed. Jeremy Cherfas, 1995, Henry Doubleday Research Association
Gives details and suppliers of 1500 fruits and 3000 vegetables.

The Seed Search
Compiled, edited and published in 1997 by Karen Platt, 37 Melbourn
Road, Crookes, Sheffield S10 1NR
This Directory provides information about the sources of 33,000 seeds,
including many varieties which are not available from commercial
companies.

Garden Seed Inventory
Seed Saver Publications (*Seed Savers Exchange, North Winn Road, Decorah,
Iowa 52101*)
Comprehensive inventory of US and Canadian mail-order seed catalogues,
the essential guide to suppliers of all open-pollinated vegetable seeds.

Seed Saving

The Seed Saver's Handbook
Jeremy Cherfas, Jude and Michel Fanton, 1996, Grover Books
A clear and thorough guide to the practicalities of growing vegetables from
home-saved seed. Suitable for beginners and more experienced seed savers.

Seed to Seed
Suzanne Ashworth, 1991, Seed Savers Publications (Seed Savers Exchange)
available through Ecologic Books in the UK
The most complete seed saving guide for 160 crops. Written for the US,
but also largeley appropriate for Europe, an invaluable reference book for
beginners or experienced seed savers.

Breed your own Vegetables
Carol Deppe, 1993, Little, Brown
This book was also written for the US, but is relevant for Europe too. It
clearly explains the basics of plant breeding to allow you to breed and save
your own strains of vegetables.

THE ISSUES

The Threatened Gene: Food politics and the loss of genetic diversity
Cary Fowler and Pat Mooney, 1991, Lutterworth Press
Required reading for those concerned with the future of gardening and the
planet. Compelling arguments by two influential agricultural activists as to
why we must conserve varieties and save our own seeds .

Saving the Seed: Genetic diversity and European agriculture
Rene Vellvé, 1992, Earthscan Publications
This clearly outlines the issues surrounding diversity and destruction in the
European Community.

Growing Diversity: Genetic resources and local food security
ed D. Cooper, Rene Vellvé, H. Hobbelink, 1992, Intermediate Technology
Publications
Activists present their experiences of managing plant genetic resources.

The Life Industry: Biodiversity, people and profits
M. Baumann, J. Bell, M. Pimbert, F. Koechlin, 1996, Intermediate
Technology Publications
Presents some of the arguments from the leading experts in the field.

*People, Plants and Patents: the impact of intellectual property on biodiversity,
conservation, trade and rural society*
Crucible Group, 1994, International Development Research Centre,
Ottawa [available through Intermediate Technology]
Identifies and examines the major issues and the range of policy alternatives.

Cultivating Knowledge: Genetic diversity, farmer experimentation and crop research
W. de Boef, K. Amanor, K. Wellard, A. Bebbington, 1993, Intermediate
Technology Publications
Worldwide case studies show the importance of smallscale farmers and local
communities in maintaining crop diversity.

Bringing Rio Home: biodiversity in our food and farming
R. Jenkins, 1992, SAFE Alliance, 21 Tower Street, London WC2H 9HS,

*Thought for Food: a briefing paper on the need to preserve the genetic diversity of our
food production system*
C. Emerson, R. Jenkins, R, 1995, SAFE Alliance

Seeds of Change: The Living Treasure
Ken Ausabel, 1994, Harper Collins
This inspiring book discusses the passionate story of the growing movement
to restore biodiversity and to raise public awareness of the issues surrounding genetic diversity.

Farmers, Plant Breeders and Seed Regulations: an issue of control
Tracey Clunies-Ross, 1996, The Ecologist, Bath Road, Sturminster
Newton, Dorset DT10 1DU

Seeds, Crops and Vulnerability: a re-examination of diversity in British agriculture
Tracey Clunies-Ross, 1995, The Ecologist

GENERAL INFORMATION

Edible Plants of the World
A.H. Sturtevant, ed. U.P. Hedrick, 1972, (originally published 1919),
Dover Books
Originally published in 1919, this invaluable reference work gives detailed
biological information about edible plants throughout the world, including
origins, and growing conditions.

The Vegetable Garden
M.M. Vilmorin-Andrieux, 1992 (first published 1885), Ten Speed Press
A classic of horticultural literature, describing cultivation techniques that
predate chemical gardening, and describing an astonishing array of varieties,
many now lost.

New Oxford Book of Food Plants
J.G. Vaughan and Catharine Geissler, 1997, Oxford University Press
An update of the original 1969 book.

The Chelsea Gardener by Philip Miller 1691-1771
H. le Rougetel, 1990, The Natural History Museum
Another classic of gardening literature, this describes techniques and
varieties from the 17th to 18th centuries.

Seed Time: the history of Essex seeds, E. Roper, 1989, Phillimore & Co Ltd,
Shopwyke Hall, Chichester, Sussex PO20 6BQ

Taylor's Guide to Heirloom Vegetables
Benjamin Watson, 1996, Houghton Mifflin, available in the UK from
Ecologic Books
A comprehensive illustrated guide to 500 historic varieties, including
instructions on how to select and grow the best heirlooms for your garden.

Field and Garden Vegetables of America,
Franklyn Burr, originally published in 1863, the facsimile edition of this
famous American directory is available in the UK from Future Foods (*see
Resources, page 173*).

Vegetables
Roger Phillips and Martyn Rix, 1995, Macmillan Reference
Over 650 vegetables that can be cultivated in a temperate climate,
illustrated with colour photographs.

Oriental Vegetables
Joy Larkcom, 1991, John Murray
The best reference work on the subject, borne out of Joy Larkcom's extensive travels through Asia, and her success in growing many Oriental varieties in the UK.

The Story of the Potato
Alan Wilson, 1993, Alan Wilson, Fleet
A detailed description of the history of the potato, its travels and development worldwide, including interesting varietal information.

Jane Grigson's Vegetable Book,
Jane Grigson, 1978, Penguin Books
A vegetable cookery book with history, anecdotes and traditional recipes.

OTHER BOOKS BY SUE STICKLAND

Greenhouses: natural vegetables, fruit and flowers all the year round
1993, Search Press and the HDRA
A guide to organic greenhouse gardening.

The Small Ecological Garden
1996, Search Press
A beginner's guide to creating an ecological garden in which both plants and wildlife thrive.

Organic Gardening
with Pauline Pears, 1995, Mitchell Beazley
A thoroughly practical and comprehensive book on organic gardening techniques.

INDEX

Entries in **bold** refer to **Directory** entries; numerals in *italic* refer to illustrations.

187

MORE TITLES FROM GAIA BOOKS

THE GARDEN HEALER
Helen Farmer-Knowles

£12.99
ISBN 1 85675 059 0

How to choose, cultivate, and care for plants in the garden to provide oils, creams and decoctions for maintaining health and beauty, and for healing simple disorders and common ailments.

THE ROTHSCHILD GARDENS
Miriam Rothschild, Kate Garton, Lionel de Rothschild
Photography by Andrew Lawson

£25.00 Hardback
ISBN 1 85675 092 2

The story of the Rothschild family's passion for gardening, from humble beginnings in the Frankfurt ghetto through to the splendour of the great mansions and châteaux in Europe, to the breathtaking informality of Miriam Rothschild's conservation gardens in Northamptonshire.

THE NATURAL GARDEN BOOK
Gardening in harmony with nature
Peter Harper, Jeremy Light and Chris Madsen

£18.99 Hardback
ISBN 1 85675 085 X

£14.99 Paperback
ISBN 1 85675 056 6

This comprehensive book provides a fresh, practical and inspiring guide to creating a productive, healthy garden, using natural gardening techniques.

G IS FOR ECOGARDEN
Nigel Dudley and Sue Stickland

£4.99
ISBN 1 85675 035 3

An A-Z of information on everything ecological: from composts and green manures to plants that attract beneficial insects, and natural predators.

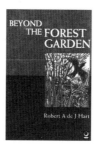

BEYOND THE FOREST GARDEN
Robert A de J Hart

£8.99
ISBN 1 85675 037 X

Inspired by the insights of artists, scientists, philosophers and healers, this work provides a blueprint for a healthy life. The book developed out of Robert Hart's own healing experiences and his forest garden in Shropshire.

THE NATURAL HEDGEHOG
Lenni Sykes with Jane Durrant

£8.99
ISBN 1 85675 042 6

Curl up with this highly illustrated guide to hedgehog care. Learn how to make your garden hedgehog-friendly and how to look after sick and injured hedgehogs.

To request a full catalogue of titles published by Gaia Books please call 01453 752985, fax 01453 752987 or write to Gaia Books Limited, 20 High Street, Stroud, Gloucestershire, GL5 1AS
e-mail address gaiabook@star.co.uk Internet address http://www.gaiabooks.co.uk